A Glimpse of Grace

[A True Story]

A Glimpse of Grace

Mary Forsythe
with Beth Clark

For information contact:
Kingdom Living Press
P.O. Box 703685
Dallas, Texas 75370
www.kingdomliving.com

International Standard Book Number: 0-9725683-0-1

Cover design by Vision Communications – Dallas

Printed in the United States of America
2 3 4 5 6 7   07 06 05 04 03

Contents

Prologue

I'll never forget the day I watched hope come alive as I sat on the concrete floor of a meeting room in northeast India, in a village so small it did not even warrant a dot on the map when I tried to locate it.

Mary Forsythe and I were part of a small teaching team from the United States, all of us so far from home that had we traveled much farther east, we would have been headed west again. We were strangers in a foreign land, surrounded by cordial men and gracious women adorned in the most beautiful fabrics we had ever seen. We did not speak a single word of their language and were only vaguely familiar with their customs and their culture. I was certain that our lives and theirs could not have been more different and wondered what we Americans could possibly say to bridge the gap.

I shouldn't have been concerned. After all, Mary was going to tell her story. I knew it well. I had heard her share it in a variety of settings—in television studios with cameras rolling and in airplanes at 37,000 feet above ground; over business dinners in crowded restaurants and with friends in the privacy of a living room; from public platforms and from makeshift pulpits behind prison doors—and had always been astounded by the responses it received.

But this time, from my seat on the floor in the Himalayan foothills, I was a bit skeptical as she began to speak through an interpreter and tell several hundred people about her life. I wondered if anyone in rural India could relate to her big-city adventures, the affluence she had acquired and lost and her journey through the United States judicial system. But as she spoke, heads started to nod as people identified with her experiences and emotions and the almost insurmountable obstacles she had overcome.

And then it happened. They caught it. Like a center fielder in perfect position, they caught the hope that landed in their hearts as they listened to Mary's amazing tale.

They knew something fundamental—that everyone can hurt, that despair does not discriminate and that devastation can strike anyone. They also knew they were listening to a woman who told them the truth, a woman who had emerged victorious after everything she had endured. They knew that, despite cultural and economic differences, the lessons of Mary's story could make a difference in their lives.

This riveting account of one woman's life leaps language barriers and transcends cultures; it reaches across all ages and stages of life because there is something in it for just about everyone. Everyone, that is, who has ever known the pain of separation and loss, everyone who has ever been alone or afraid, everyone who has ever dealt with one disappointment after another or stared life in the face and admitted, "I can't do this anymore."

Experience, especially when it is difficult, breeds compassion. But victory over difficult experiences also breeds determination to help others apprehend the truths that lead to triumph. That's the power of this story. As you read it, don't be surprised if you find yourself laughing, if you find yourself crying, and by the time you finish, if you find yourself changed.

Beth Clark
Nashville, TN

Chapter 1

The Verdict

"Mary, it's time."

My attorney gathered his papers—and I tried to gather my composure—as we prepared to walk toward the courtroom to hear the verdict to be returned in my case. When we arrived, I took a deep breath that felt as though it could have been my last, and followed him into the room. If atmospheres could speak, that one would have screamed hatred.

As I made my way to the defense table, my eyes darted around the courtroom. It was packed with people representing a variety of government agencies, such as the Texas Department of Health and Human Resources, the Texas State Board of Pharmacy and federal agents from Washington, D.C. The looks of hostile anticipation on their faces indicated that they might burst into celebration if I were convicted of the charges against me and against the small pharmacy I owned—fifteen felony counts ranging from mail fraud to theft of government property.

In the same visual sweep, I saw my parents sitting on the back row—and the looks on their faces indicated that their hearts would crumble into a million pieces if I were found guilty. I was thirty-one years old, no longer their little girl, but still wishing they could rescue me. I was in great-big, grown-up trouble—these were white-collar federal offenses we were dealing with. My parents were powerless to help me, and I was powerless to help myself.

My immediate future had been determined by a jury, twelve total strangers who had watched and listened for the past three-and-a-half-weeks as it felt like everything I had ever done was pulled out into the shining light of day and paraded before them. My mistakes were on public display and my every weakness was mercilessly examined and ridiculed. I did not know how anyone else felt, but for me, observing the court proceedings was like watching a movie of my life and sitting next to the critics.

Now that the trial was finished and the jury's deliberations complete, they had made up their collective mind— and would pronounce me either innocent or guilty. It was time for me to find out.

Judge John Faulk instructed me to stand as the members of the jury entered the courtroom. With my heart thundering in my chest and my entire body drenched in a cold sweat, I watched the jurors file into their places. *They don't have good news*, I thought. I could tell because none of them would make eye contact with me.

Two of my pharmacy employees had been tried as co-defendants along with me and their verdicts were read first. "We the jury find the defendant, Rachel Gardener, innocent on all counts," said the foreman. He read the same statement again, using the name of my other employee. "We the jury find the defendant, Leah Finley, innocent on all counts."

Then it was my turn. The entire scene fell into slow

motion as I watched the foreman hand my verdict to the judge, who unfolded it and silently read its brief contents. With a nod, Judge Faulk returned the paper to the foreman, who finally announced: "We the jury find the defendant, Mary Elizabeth Forsythe, guilty on all counts."

Nothing in the world can prepare a person to hear her own name and then the word *guilty*. And nothing could have prepared me to hear what I heard next—my mother, as she began to wail from the pit of her soul. It was primal, and it came from a place deep inside of her, a place I did not even know existed. I found out what agony sounds like as I heard her voice—the voice that had soothed me and scolded me, the voice that had brought me both comfort and correction. Over the course of my life, I had given this woman both pride and pain. I had brought her great delight and deep disappointment. But nothing in days gone by could have prepared either of us for the instant she heard that I had been found guilty.

I screamed from the defense table, "Mother! Mother! It'll be all right! I promise you! It will be all right!" I had said those words so many times before, and they had proven true. But it would be a long, long time before she or I would know that it really would be all right, and my entire life would have to be turned inside out.

My attorney took my arm in an attempt to quiet me. I slumped into my chair, with fear and bitterness and disbelief all raging inside of me. Then I went completely numb. The pressure of a two-and-a-half-year legal investigation had been so intense, but I had held up under it. The stress of the trial had been so great, but I had withstood it. The torment inside of me had been vicious, but somehow I had managed to keep from falling apart.

Now it was over.

Summoning enough strength to send a visual hate message to those who convicted me, I gazed straight into the eyes of the judge and the jurors with a look of pure venom. I did not know I was capable of loathing so quickly and so intensely, but in that moment, anger and hatred inhabited me and I despised those jurors and Judge John Faulk with diabolic force.

The range of emotion in the courtroom spanned from jubilation to devastation. On one side, the prosecuting attorneys and representatives from state and federal agencies rejoiced to see me convicted for what they considered my deliberate deceit of the government concerning the oversight of a contract to dispense a particular prescription drug. On the other side of the room, my two employees stood with their families and friends hugging, crying tears of happiness and heaving with sighs of relief.

And then there were my parents. Looking past the elation of the prosecutors and my co-defendants, I saw them, emotionally obliterated by the blow the jury had dealt them by declaring me guilty. My father's strong arms encircled my mother as she lay against him, curled in a fetal position, consumed by the unique devastation and grief only a mother can feel. His arms formed a shield around her body, but they could not hold her heart.

I responded differently, however, and shifted into a coping mechanism with which I had a long history—denial. I knew how to mentally escape reality under the kind of pressure I faced that day, so I simply chose not to comprehend the gravity of my circumstances, nor to dwell on how deeply I hated the jurors. Instead, I listened as the judge adjourned the court, then I reassured my mother and went back to work that afternoon.

The guilty verdict meant at least two things: that my pharmacy would have to be closed, and that I could be sentenced to as many as seven years in federal prison. All I could think was, *But I'm not a criminal! I didn't even mean to do anything wrong!* I didn't want to leave the career I loved, and I certainly didn't want to go to prison. I had to ask myself how on earth I ever ended up in so much trouble.

Chapter 2

Starting Out

I never really was a small-town girl. Although I was raised in a delightful rural paradise nestled in the heart of western Kentucky, I always dreamed of spending my life in the city. The gentle pace and charm of our little spot on the map were well-suited for many of its residents, including my parents, whose roots had reached deep into the bluegrass hills for generations.

Like their parents before them, my mother and dad wanted to raise their children in a town filled with front porches and fertile farmland and family nearby. And so, by 1960, when my arrival completed our family of four, we were poised to follow the pattern of so many others in our coal-mining community. My mother busied herself with a multitude of civic activities; my dad worked hard to provide for us; and my older sister and I spent our days growing up in the safe, carefree environment of the pleasant place we called home.

A tall, solid, steadfast man of few words but wonderful dry wit, my dad had the gift of "being there" for my sister and me. Whether he was cheering us on at a sporting event or letting us crank the freezer to complete his world's best homemade ice cream or taking us to fish in a nearby pond, we were often together. During the week, he worked for the local Chevrolet dealer, but during his free time, he exercised his amazing green thumb growing tomatoes, tending our apple trees and keeping our lawn manicured to perfection.

My mother usually started her days with an early-morning round of golf and, once she had completed her eighteen holes, she was off to the church or the library or the hospital for volunteer work. But her community involvement never took priority over her family. No matter what she did, she made life lively for us and always found something to be excited about. With a great big generous heart, she was often the first person to arrive with a meal on the doorstep of the sick or the bereaved. A ready laugh was never far from her lips and her positive attitude seemed to rub off on everyone around her. She approached everything with a "can-do" mentality—even the often-daunting task of keeping up with me!

I was born busy. Even in pictures as a toddler, I was either squirming out of someone's arms or standing on someone's lap, looking ready to jump and unwilling to be still long enough for a split-second shutter snap! Before I could walk, I appeared to be tailor-made for the fast lane.

For years, I never visited a city larger than Louisville. But somehow I knew a whole world existed beyond our little town, beyond Louisville, beyond anywhere I had ever been—and I longed for a life that was larger and busier than anything my natural eyes had ever seen.

I countered the relaxed rhythm of the place I lived with homemade excitement. I was industrious, resourceful, creative, mischievous at times and always brimming with initiative. Whenever I found myself at a loss for something to do, I invented something that was, at least in my mind, challenging and stimulating and wonderful. And it usually involved one of two things: science or making money. Naturally inquisitive, I gravitated toward all things scientific. I started by collecting bugs and then progressed through several chemistry sets, each one more advanced than its predecessor. But what I really wanted was a microscope—a *real* microscope—and as soon as my parents felt I was old enough, they presented me with one as a Christmas gift. I spent hours with one of my big brown eyes tightly shut and the other wide open, peering down the microscope's lens into the unseen wonders of an insect wing or a piece of a flower or a drop of water or something from the refrigerator.

I was not only a budding scientist, but also a miniature entrepreneur. Always looking for something to sell so that I could earn my own money, I started by making fudge and lemonade in my parents' kitchen. Each week, with a card table, a small metal chair, and a hand-written sign, I set up shop on our front lawn. At the end of each "business" day, I deposited my earnings in a jar in my bedroom and watched with great pleasure as my funds increased.

Finally, when I was thirteen years old, the day came when I could combine my two favorite interests. Ruth and George Miller, who owned our town pharmacy on Main Street, offered me my first job—wrapping presents during Christmas holidays. I quickly developed a genuine interest in the pharmacy, and the Millers indulged and encouraged my scientific curiosity as I watched them fill prescriptions and couldn't help but overhear conversations about rashes and sniffles and stomach aches. Never a casual observer, I paid careful attention to the activities of the store, and when no customers were present, I bombarded the Millers with questions about medicine and chemistry and the human body. I enjoyed gift-wrapping and welcomed the chance to earn an hourly wage, but it was being around prescriptions and antibiotics and other concoctions that I *really* loved.

After Christmas that year, the Millers extended my part-time employment and paid me to do odd jobs around the pharmacy that so captivated me. By the time I was fourteen, I was beginning to grasp certain aspects of being a pharmacist and, as best I could, had come to appreciate the Millers' knowledge and skill. I had also saved enough money to accomplish one of my first financial goals—a purchase on the stock market.

I did not know how to buy stock, but knew exactly where to go for help. I counted my savings one afternoon and lugged my jar full of money from my bedroom to my grandmother's house. As a young woman in the 1920s, my grandmother had attended a prestigious East Coast university and was educated beyond most of the women of her day. This stately, dignified woman not only had a soft spot in her heart for her grandchildren, she also had her own investments. She graciously agreed to assist me when I presented her with my jar and proudly said, "Grandmother, here's all the money I've got. I want to put it in the stock market. What do I do?"

After we reviewed some information on various companies, she helped me choose a stock, and I entrusted my life's savings to her. She bought the stock in my name and gave me the certificate when it arrived in the mail. I felt an unusual sense of accomplishment as I read the stock certificate closely and said to myself with pleasure, *This might be my first investment, but it won't be my last!*

I continued to work at the pharmacy after school, on

Saturdays and during summers until I finished high school. After all that experience, I knew what I wanted to do with my life—I wanted to be a pharmacist.

When I began to investigate colleges, I was thrilled to discover that the University of Kentucky in Lexington was not only the school I had always wanted to attend, but was also home to one of the top-ranked pharmacy schools in the United States. My plans for a wonderful life were made: I would go to the University of Kentucky, study hard, earn a pharmacy degree, pass my board exams and become a pharmacist. Then I would finally be able to move to a big city and take advantage of everything it had to offer. Little did I know that, before my wonderful life unfolded, some things would take advantage of me. Beyond the boundaries of my quaint, innocent hometown, I would find a cruel and confusing world.

When I burst on the scene at the University of Kentucky, I thoroughly enjoyed my newfound freedom from parental supervision and availed myself of the many social opportunities college afforded. The intensity with which I had always approached life stayed with me: I studied hard, and I played hard. Part of my playing hard included an increase in alcohol use, with which I had experimented in high school. But once I got to college it quickly became as much a part of my life as attending class or preparing for a test.

Like many female college freshmen, I had looked forward to joining a sorority and was so excited about going through the process required for membership. I knew precisely which of those exclusive clubs I wanted to join and soon made friends with as many members as possible. I was not concerned, though, because I was a "chapter legacy" in that sorority and because of strong family and social connections there, my acceptance was almost guaranteed.

But the sorority did not extend an invitation to me. In fact, I was "black-balled," which meant that they made a pro-active, intentional decision to exclude me from the group I had set my heart on. I was shocked and embarrassed and confused.

Nothing shouted "Loser" more than being black-balled—and I never lost at anything! Whether it was a Girl Scout cookie sale, a high school tennis match or a fund-raising contest for the school band, I won. I *always* won.

Beneath the feeling of defeat, being rejected by the sorority only served to reinforce something I had struggled with all of my life—the feeling that no one really wanted me, that I was not worthy of affection or acceptance.

I had always been surrounded by family and friends who loved me in a million ways, so I did not understand why I had always perceived rejection or what had fueled those feelings. But because I wrestled with them, I had spent many years learning to compensate for them by nurturing an unusual degree of personal pride, over-achieving and staying extremely busy. In the aftermath of my rejection by the sorority, I resorted to those familiar coping mechanisms and topped them off with an alcohol habit that became a *bona fide* problem by the end of my freshman year.

When classes resumed the following fall, I devoted my energies to new courses, homework, an active social life and more drinking. Feelings of rejection still festered deep inside me, but I was improving my ability to hide them from others and deny them to myself. As I fell into the routine of my sophomore year, I was beginning to feel better about who I was—at least I appeared to. I covered up my feelings of worthlessness with a shallow self-confidence that few people saw through. And just as I was gaining proficiency in my masquerade, something terrible happened.

A young man I considered an acquaintance, but not a friend, gave me a ride to a party. He needed to stop by his apartment first, he said, and invited me to wait for him inside instead of in the car. In my naive innocence, I followed him into his apartment. Suddenly, and against my fiercest resistance, he raped me.

I took hot showers for days.

I had never been sexually active in any way, and that brutal experience left me physically shocked and emotionally shattered, completely debilitated. Not only did he rape me; he murdered something deep inside of me—something invisible, something in my soul.

All the feelings of rejection I had struggled with in the past suddenly took on an almost supernatural dimension. They spoke to me constantly, sneering at me and even blaming me as they carried out a taunting celebration of my filth and worthlessness. If ever there had been even an ember of hope for overcoming my rejection, it was extinguished. It was not glowing; it was not smoking; it was nothing more than cold, gray ash.

I did not tell anyone what happened—I *could* not—but was too traumatized and too ashamed to stay in school. I was unable to face anyone, unable to concentrate on my studies, and unable to enjoy anything, so I decided to run away.

With that decision made, I called my grandmother, informed her that I needed to leave school and asked her for some money. Naturally, she would not agree to give me it to me until I explained the reason for such an uncharacteristic request. Because the embarrassment of telling her what had happened to me surpassed the shame of staying in school, I didn't run away after all.

Through the months that followed, no matter what I did, I could not escape the utter humiliation and inner torment that accompanied me. They settled into a seat in the pit of my wounded heart and never left. I never looked them in the eye, never challenged them, never tried to evict them from my heart. I just hurt. I did not know where to turn for help or how to ask for it, and I could not convince myself that I was not ruined forever. So I dealt with the profound ache inside of me the only way I could—by crawling into a den of denial with my dark secret and its riveting pain. And I hoped no one would ever find me.

Somehow, over the course of my remaining college semesters, I managed to resume my studies, to maintain an acceptable grade point average and to graduate. Armed with my pharmacy degree and a passing score on my board exams, I was ready to make my mark on the world, to embark on the life I had always wanted and to leave my past far behind me. Little did I know—my past could not, *would* not, stay where I wanted to leave it.

Chapter 3

The Downward Spiral

My first full-time job. I had looked forward to it for years. A major chain drug store hired me not only to fill prescriptions but also to manage their pharmacy, which enabled me to both practice my chosen profession and sharpen my retail skills. There was only one drawback: the job required me to live in Lexington, which prohibited my moving to the big, bustling city of my dreams. Nevertheless, the job was a good one, and I knew that it would enable me to get established in my career so I could relocate later.

With a regular paycheck at my disposal, I continued investing in the stock market and found myself making one profitable pick after another. Before long, I had financial resources that far exceeded the income of any pharmacist I had ever known. With a good salary and phenomenal investment success, the pieces of my up-and-coming life were beginning to fall into place, with one exception—I wanted someone to share it with.

Several months later, I met a dashing young British man

whose life seemed lifted straight out of a storybook. Henry Hendrickson was charming, cultured, well-connected and came complete with a family castle in the English countryside. His business pursuits in the horse racing industry brought him to Lexington for the famous thoroughbred sales, but a common cold brought him into the pharmacy one afternoon.

Instant attraction led to a long-term, long-distance relationship that included, for me, weekend get-aways to London, exposure to the wealth-driven equine business and opportunities to enjoy the privilege that accompanied Henry's position in society. I was taken by that lifestyle and strove to imitate it in every possible way. With my quick trips to Europe and my foreign romantic interest, I was becoming something I'd always wanted to be—a jet-setter.

But underneath this seemingly glamorous existence, I was still raw from the trauma of a few hideous moments in the apartment of a young man I barely knew. In an attempt to rid myself of the shame I could not shake, I unknowingly sought refuge in my relationship with Henry and in the silly fact that I personally possessed and controlled a considerable amount of money for someone my age. It was not long before my faulty fortress began to crumble. My relationship with my British boyfriend ended, and I was left alone. In the wake of our breakup and with a persistent ache in my heart, I decided to act on my life-long dream of venturing outside of Kentucky.

I needed a fresh start. Perhaps I could forget what happened to me in college and the feelings of rejection that dogged me if I moved out of state and simply got away from the place where it all happened. Besides, I had always wanted to go to the big city—where the lights were brighter, the pace was faster, the competition was fiercer and the opportunities were greater. I wanted to embrace the professional potential, the social life and the general activity of a major metropolis. I was looking for the busiest, glitziest place I could find—and in the 1980s, no place was more attractive to me than Dallas, Texas.

Arriving in Dallas under the incorrect impression that my life would finally begin to change for the better, I landed a job in a drug store whose clientele included successful business men and women, well-known artists and a number of wealthy, influential people. My fascination with impressive-looking possessions increased exponentially as I encountered the world of expensive cars and exclusive neighborhoods. But the entrepreneur in me would not rest, so I opened a sideline business as a pharmaceutical consultant. When I looked at my life after a few months in Dallas, I was quite proud of myself. After all, for a young woman, I had done well. Having decided that I had earned the right to gloat a little bit, and never slow to look down my nose at the next person, I developed enough arrogance to cover all of Texas!

But beneath the haughtiness, I was still trying to outrun the pain that always caught up with me. I was absolutely driven in all the wrong directions, in hot pursuit of things that only aggravated my inner agony. Nevertheless, I had gone to Dallas for a new beginning, so I stayed in costume, playing the role of the young capitalist just waiting for the right moment to leap up the professional ladder to land on the rung of my dreams: owning my own pharmacy.

One day, opportunity knocked. A local physician was opening a new clinic and offered me the chance to have my own small pharmacy in his building. I was ripe for the challenge. Because I genuinely enjoyed my work and cared about the people I served, I had developed a rapport with many of my clients at the chain drug store and enjoyed a reputation for exceptional service. For that reason, many of those customers transferred their business to my pharmacy when it opened.

I was in my element. My fledgling enterprise only consisted of a walk-up window, through which I received and dispensed prescriptions, and a small storage area. Furnished with gray metal shelves I assembled myself and stocked with all the medications I needed, my first pharmacy was off to a strong start. With me as its sole employee, this undertaking demanded most of my time and all of my energy. Not only was I the pharmacist, I was also the janitor, the window-cleaner and the clerk. But business began to boom. Before long, I was filling more than one hundred prescriptions per day and was able to hire a part-time employee.

Within several years, I had purchased a home in Dallas' elite, historic Highland Park neighborhood and paid cash for a sleek, black Mercedes convertible. I wore designer clothes, attended fashionable parties and ended most of my days with a glass of the finest champagne. I was also romantically involved with a handsome, successful bachelor named Mike, who had everything I thought I wanted.

Mike was a true Renaissance man, equally comfortable at the ballet in a tuxedo as at the rodeo in faded jeans and cowboy boots. His keen financial expertise, administrative skills and social graces made him respected in the business community. But what attracted me to this dark-haired, dark-eyed gentleman was the way he exuded both confidence and compassion and the way he could be simultaneously so intense and so much fun. Rugged and romantic, one of the things Mike enjoyed most was saddling up his Arabian horses for us and leading me on a leisurely sunset ride around his sprawling ranch near Ft. Worth. Afterward, the two of us often savored a glass of wine while we cooked dinner, which usually included wild game from one of Mike's hunting adventures.

With what appeared to be a fairytale courtship and startling business success, I looked like I had "arrived" and was living the American dream. But inside, I still ached. Eventually, I realized that moving to Dallas had not healed me and that a change of address had not changed anything inside of me at all. Nothing I had done or acquired had been able to release me from the torment of my past. As proud as I was of my accomplishments and as happy as I was with Mike, my entire being was still wrapped with layers of shame. No one knew how miserable I was, and for the next year I continued to live under the ruthless rule of believing that nothing could or would *ever* change.

About that time, I moved my pharmacy to a new location, and many established clients followed me. The business and my consulting services continued to thrive, and these endeavors, coupled with more stock market success, produced burgeoning bank accounts that impressed even me. My unusual gift for earning and managing money had never left me: I enjoyed making it; I enjoyed watching it multiply; and I enjoyed spending it. A lesson kept trying to teach itself to me, but I could not seem to learn: money has no power to heal.

Eventually resigned to the fact that finances could not fix me, I was compelled to look elsewhere for something that really could help. In the course of my business dealings, I met a wealthy, elegant European couple named Vincent and Katrina, and we became fast friends. Both several years older than I, they had sparkling personalities and were creative thinkers and gifted conversationalists. I was attracted to their genuine warmth and loved listening to the beautiful accents with which they spoke. Everything about their lives emanated style and artistry, and everything about them fascinated me, so I began spending as much time with them as possible, gleaning all I could from their worldly experience and business acumen. Even though they were cosmopolitan in their lifestyle and global in their financial interests, they took a personal, almost parental, interest in me.

Not only did these two people introduce me to their professional and social pursuits; they also introduced me to something that seemed to promise the healing and relief my life had made me desperate for. Because Vincent was a marvelous chef and Katrina was a wonderful hostess, they often treated their friends to fabulous dinner parties. On one such evening, a guest complained of a migraine headache. Excusing herself from the table, Janet informed us that she needed to leave and go to bed immediately. Vincent asked her to stay and announced that he could cure her headache.

I was intrigued. As a pharmacist, I knew Janet was right and that she would not find quick relief from her pain. At that time, medicine offered little hope for migraine headaches, so I wondered what Vincent might possibly know about treating them that I did not.

After convincing Janet not to leave, he went into his office, but quickly returned to the dining room with a long, brown leather pouch from which he removed two thin, white crystal rods. He pointed one rod toward each of her temples and began to speak words that were soothing, but authoritative, at the same time. To my utter amazement, her headache disappeared instantly.

With a chant, two crystal rods and a healed headache, I was hooked. I began to read books that explained and encouraged New Age and "white magic" practices and continued to be fascinated by crystals. I watched Vincent use them on other people, allowed him to teach me how to use them and even attended a crystal show with Katrina at a Dallas hotel. With my involvement in it, the New Age found not only a committed follower, but a terrific promoter. I was so captivated by these supernatural practices that I began sharing my experiences with many friends, giving them books, teaching tapes and all sorts of New Age paraphernalia.

Part of my personal public relations campaign for the New Age reached into my professional life. Because my pharmacy was one of a very few that distributed AZT, a purported "miracle drug" for the HIV virus, a large clientele of HIV/AIDS patients looked to my store to meet all their pharmaceutical needs. I could hardly bear to see people ravaged by that disease, weaker and more frail every time they picked up a prescription. In my zeal to see them helped, I wondered, *If Vincent can heal a migraine headache with crystal rods, what can he do for HIV?* I sent several of my clients to him, hoping desperately that he could cure them.

Meanwhile, I continued to be drawn into the New Age belief system and the supernatural power within it. But I ran into a problem as I followed that path. I would not have admitted it, but knew in the core of my being that something about it was not right because I kept my New Age interests and involvement hidden from Mike. I made sure that no books or other tools of the trade were visible in my home when he was there, and never spoke to him about that aspect of my life. I knew he would not approve and would try to talk me out of it. I did not want to be talked out of it, but as I continued to pursue New Age powers and practices, I was gradually forced to accept the disappointing truth that, like money, this religion had no power to heal my heart.

Chapter 4

Real Trouble

I was a study in paradox. There I was, in the business of health and healing, but personally unable to recover from the heart-injuries that festered in me like untreated wounds. To the average observer, I looked "together," but in reality I was falling apart—and my professional life only exacerbated my personal pain.

Where my small pharmacy was once a dream come true for me, it became a nightmare during the late 1980s, when AIDS was the focus of much public attention in the United States. The drug AZT was in high demand and had only recently been released from experimental status, so the United States government provided it through state programs. My pharmacy was chosen as one of the official state dispensaries and in fact, after the county hospital in Dallas, my little drug store was Texas' largest AZT distributor.

Because pharmacy audits are not unusual, I was not alarmed one crisp fall morning in 1989 when three agents from the Texas Department of Health and Human Resources walked into my store, flashed their badges and stated the purpose of their visit: to audit my inventory records. I provided them with a work space in the back office, began collecting the information they requested and even offered to buy their lunch.

They were awfully serious, even cold, as they began their work, and I discovered early in their visit that they had come to investigate one specific aspect of my business—the government contract to dispense AZT. I stayed with them in the office, watching as they quietly and soberly reviewed inventory records—and wondering, *Why does this audit seem unusually intense? What is really going on here? And why don't they just relax?*

The audit came on the heels of a national wave of health insurance fraud schemes. Medical insurance issues had been in the spotlight often, and the regulatory agencies were extra diligent as they monitored state and federal programs involving healthcare providers and the pharmaceutical industry. As I observed the agents' silent, meticulous work, I mentally reviewed everything I had done in regard to the AZT contract and thought about how stressful the pharmacy had become since we started dispensing the drug.

AZT was terribly expensive and few people could afford to pay full price, but the state program provided a thirty-day supply to eligible patients for a co-payment of five dollars. In addition, private insurance carriers covered part of the cost of the drug, and as a service to our patients, we billed insurance companies directly and handled the administrative details of filing claims and collecting payments.

The clerk kept inventory records for the state program in a simple color-coded index card system. We ordered the AZT that was dispensed through the state program from the state, and we ordered the AZT that was covered by private insurance carriers from a different supplier. In the beginning, we separated the inventories from each vendor and kept them in different areas of the pharmacy, but eventually all of the AZT stock ended up together.

Our system was frustrated by the fact that some patients left their doctors' offices with two AZT prescriptions—one to be billed to an insurance company and one to be billed to the state program. When presented with two prescriptions signed by a physician, we filled both—a practice that was technically permissible, but ethically questionable. What complicated matters further, however, was that some patients presented prescriptions with aliases on them, so we sometimes ended up with two sets of records that were actually for the same patient. Trying to keep track of state-program patients who had multiple names or multiple prescriptions and those who were in and out of the hospital or deceased without our knowledge created administrative chaos.

In the frenzy of our business, we estimated the amount of AZT needed to fill prescriptions each week and ordered enough from the state to meet our projected demand instead of waiting until patients came into the pharmacy with prescriptions in hand. Occasionally, we placed orders for state-program patients before we were notified that they had died because we assumed they would need another month's supply. When the state AZT provider examined our orders and realized they had sent us medicine for a deceased person, they called us, brought the matter to our attention and indicated that they would just "short" our next order. Even so, we often ended up with excess inventory.

These problems occurred frequently enough to catch the careful eye of a state auditor. Without my knowledge, the government had begun to keep a close watch on the pharmacy—and that was why the three agents showed up unexpectedly at my store. They had arrived on a mission and left with their mission accomplished as they walked out of my pharmacy that day with documents I willfully surrendered—documents that would later be used against me in a court of law.

Soon after the agents' initial visit, one of them returned with more questions and requests for more documents. I was not glad to see her because, by that time, I had discovered that the pharmacy really did have a serious problem with AZT inventory. And by that time, I had begun to understand why.

I realized that in the midst of our bookkeeping complexity, business had exploded as word quickly spread that we dispensed the drug so many people were counting on. Word also spread that we were sensitive to the unique pharmaceutical needs of HIV patients and to the social stigma that often accompanied them. Before we knew it, people were flocking to the pharmacy. Patients came from all over Texas, and from other states, who needed the drug for medical reasons, but who also needed anonymity for professional or social reasons—and it was more than we could handle.

Helping HIV/AIDS patients was not a popular thing to do at that time, and we tried our best to serve them with dignity and kindness. Instead of simply being a place for people to find remedies for sore throats and toothaches, the pharmacy became like a lighthouse, shining beacons of encouragement in the form of blue-and-white pills and a steady stream of comforting words. Instead of just selling cold medicine or eye drops or antacids, we became dispensers of hope—which meant that a constant parade of devastated lives marched in and out of the pharmacy every single day.

The emotional aspects of serving AIDS patients were challenging enough, but dealing with the paperwork that accompanied each one had grown more and more difficult week after week. As the owner of the business, I was solely responsible for making sure that our bookkeeping was in order and that we administered the state program with integrity. I had hired and trained a competent staff to ensure that the pharmacy offered excellent service and stayed profitable, but I realized, looking back, that as the desperation of our clients increased and inventory management challenges spun out of control, I had allowed my service to the patients to outweigh my proper oversight of the business. My fatal philosophy became, "fill prescriptions first; deal with details later."

Imparting that approach by example to my staff, I had left them to manage the business while I glanced its way occasionally to make sure it was still functioning. But that was only part of my problem. I realized that I had been restless and needed a new professional mountain to climb, since I had already conquered owning my own business. Because I wanted a new challenge, I had begun to travel extensively with Mike and to think about different business avenues we might explore together. Turning my eyes and efforts in those directions, I had turned away from my obligations at the pharmacy. Although I paid my employees well, I really had expected too much of them as I left the administration of the government AZT program in their hands.

I was beginning to understand why the authorities were investigating the pharmacy, and within a few weeks of the agent's second visit, I called her and asked whether I needed to consult an attorney as a result of the audit. Her response was, "I can't advise you." And I could hear clearly what she could not say. We were indeed dealing with a serious offense, and yes, I needed an attorney. With a knot in my stomach, I contacted the State Board of Pharmacy and asked for advice and a recommendation for legal counsel. They suggested a Dallas law firm, and I promptly made an appointment with an attorney who also had a pharmacy degree and was familiar with the legal issues of our profession. When he referred me to another attorney—one who handled criminal cases—I knew I was in serious trouble.

Until that point, I had not thought the investigation was important enough to even tell Mike about it. But I recognized after talking with the attorney that it was indeed serious enough to share with him. One evening I cooked a delicious dinner, poured him a glass of his favorite red wine and set the dining room table with candles and my finest china. Even though I had set elegant tables for just the two of us many times before, that night he could sense that something was out of the ordinary.

As casually as I could, I said, "I think I've got a problem at the pharmacy." He looked at me, without a word, as if to say, "Continue." So I re-capped the events of the past few weeks. Just as I expected, he did believe the investigation was cause for concern but responded with characteristic calm and assured me that he would be there for me as I straightened it out.

He knew, as I did, that I had been living a life surrounded by death. He was familiar with some of the stories that had touched me deeply in the preceding months. He also knew that I had seen and experienced things so grievous that they had reached all the way down to the bottom of my heart and pulled out something that had been covered up and held captive by years of my own internal pain—compassion.

I could not remember exactly when or how it had happened. I just remembered gradually realizing that something stirred in me every time I poured those little pills of promise into a brown bottle and handed it to an AIDS patient. Even though the administrative aspects of dispensing AZT according to the government contract were complicated and time-consuming, I seemed to forget about the red-tape every time a patient thanked me for my help. More and more, I had been able to see beyond the medicinal needs of HIV patients and into the tragic realities of their lives.

I had gotten a vivid close-up glimpse into the impact of AIDS on a person's life when I received a phone call one afternoon from a local physician named Dr. Adams.

"Mary," he said, "I've just diagnosed an HIV patient who needs a high level of confidentiality. I've written an AZT prescription for him, but it's under an alias. Can you let him into the pharmacy after hours and fill it?"

I agreed to see Dr. Adams' patient—a tall, well-dressed man who introduced himself as "Thomas." Fully aware that I knew his name was anything but Thomas, he began to tell me his story as I filled his prescription. He lived in Washington, DC, and was known in his community as a devoted family man. For that reason, and because he held a highly visible and influential position in the city, he was unwilling to risk getting AZT from a pharmacy in his hometown. He told me that he would fly to Dallas regularly for his appointments with Dr. Adams and asked me if I would continue to supply his AZT and guarantee his anonymity. I agreed to do both.

I sent him on his way with his medication and the best pharmaceutical advice I had to offer. I left the pharmacy that evening overwhelmed by the thought that my involvement in a dark and complicated world had just intensified. I was shaken by my encounter with Thomas—a man with a family, a man with a high-paying job, a man other people respected— and asked myself, *How am I supposed to deal with this?* But I could not answer my own question, so I did what I always did when I could not process an experience—went straight home and poured myself a drink.

But that was only the beginning of a series of increasingly shocking stories in which I found myself cast in a supporting role. One day, an adorable set of twin boys I had not seen before came into the store with their mother. I smiled when I saw the toddlers and greeted the mother as she handed me two prescriptions. Expecting to need medicine for an ear infection or some other common childhood ailment, I made conversation with the mother until I actually read what the children needed and stopped as though I had been paralyzed: liquid AZT, one prescription for each little boy.

I could hardly believe both boys were suffering with AIDS, one with a more advanced case than the other. In a quick attempt to hide my grief and horror, I walked out from behind the counter and took the more lethargic child in my arms. Smiling at the mother with all the sympathy my heart could muster, I patted her son with one hand and filled the prescriptions with the other.

I could not help but wonder how two children in the same family had contracted AIDS, and I soon found out that the young mother, Margaret, and her husband had adopted the boys from overseas, thinking they were healthy babies. To their shock, the boys were infected with that hideous disease, and the couple's dreams for strong, happy sons were shattered.

One day, the father brought the boys in and as usual, I took one of them in my arms and between making silly sounds in his face, asked about Margaret. "She had to have surgery," he replied. "It was just a routine operation, though, and she'll be back on her feet in no time."

"Great." I said. "Tell her I asked about her, and let me know if we can help."

He thanked me and left the pharmacy with his sons and the medicine he hoped would prolong their lives.

A few months later, Margaret returned and I greeted her. "Glad to see you, Margaret! I heard you had surgery. How are you doing?" She simply handed me a single prescription. It was for AZT, which I expected, but it was for capsules, not liquid. It was not for one of the boys; it was for her. Noticing the questions written all over my face, she explained.

"Something went wrong during my surgery. I got AIDS through a blood transfusion." I could hardly speak, but my mind went to work immediately trying to think of ways to help. At last I said, "Margaret, I'm so sorry. Would it help if we delivered the medicine for you and the boys from now on?"

"Yes," she replied. "Thanks, Mary. It's going to get harder and harder to come here as the days go by."

Any time they needed medicine, someone from the pharmacy took it to their house. It was the least we could do.

For every Thomas, there had been countless others, and though I never met anyone whose story was as thoroughly devastating as Margaret's, one life-and-death drama after another had played itself out on the stage of my little pharmacy. I had cared, even ached, for people; and I had done all I could do for them.

Thinking about how genuine my compassion had been, I had to ask myself if my good intentions to help people were going to end up hurting me.

Chapter 5

The United States of America v. Me

My attorneys scrambled to prevent a trip to the grand jury, but I really did not understand why. I had been told that a grand jury hearing could result in an indictment, but I also thought the grand jury's function was to determine whether or not a case included enough evidence to warrant a trial. I truly believed that any reasonable grand jury would clearly see that the government did not need to take me to court. They would see that I had made mistakes, but that I certainly was not a felon and had intended no harm. *I know I've got an inventory problem,* I said to myself, *but I've also got enough money to write the government a check and cover it. Then this will all be over.*

But it was not that simple. The government refused to accept my offer to reimburse them for the amount of the inventory discrepancy and insisted upon a grand jury hearing. I learned that a grand jury only sees the evidence of the prosecution—and that was stacked heavily against me.

After the grand jury reviewed the prosecution's evidence,

they deemed a trial necessary and one afternoon at about 5:30, I received a phone call from my attorney. His words sent a chill all the way through my body. "Mary, an indictment has been handed down by the grand jury."

Not only had the grand jury indicted me individually and the pharmacy as a business entity, they had also indicted two of my employees, Rachel Gardener and Leah Finley, and filed fifteen felony charges against us. In one sense, I was terrified because I knew that, if convicted, I could go to prison. But in another sense, I was not worried at all because I had usually managed to get out of whatever trouble came my way. *No problem,* I convinced myself, *I can find a way out of this mess.*

Mike had an idea. In all seriousness, he suggested one day that we simply flee the United States and start our lives over in a foreign country. Mike was a smart man, one who tended to advise me well, and when I first heard his recommendation, it sounded appealing. He was willing to sacrifice his entire life, everything he had worked for, just to be with me—and in my estimation, *that* was true love. The more I thought about each option though, I knew I did not want to run away. Then again, neither did I want to live through the trial and potential consequences awaiting me.

Because of Mike's longing for us to begin a new life together with all of my difficulties half a world away, he made sure our passports were in order and investigated places we could go. The pressure to escape created even more internal turmoil than was already churning within me. But I kept hearing a little voice inside saying, "If you do this, you'll never see your mother and dad again." I knew that was true. If I left the country, I would not ever see them again—and that was enough to keep me in the United States, willing to face whatever I had to endure. My ultimate answer to Mike was,

"No. We're not leaving."

When I told Katrina and Vincent I had been indicted, they were concerned. But, like Mike, they had a solution. "Don't worry," they said. "We know someone who can help you." They told me about a "spiritual woman" named Jackie, who had the power to predict the future and the ability to give me insight into what the government might be plotting against me. Their idea sounded like a lifeline to me. *If I know what the government is planning*, I thought, *maybe I can stay a step ahead of them.* I agreed to see this spiritual woman, so they called her and scheduled my visit.

I was surprised as I drove into what I considered a nice neighborhood. I did not know what to expect, but I certainly did not expect Jackie's house to look so *normal.* Nervous and wondering what she would say to me, I rang the doorbell and felt as though I were about to cross the threshold into the land of hope. The woman answered the door with a friendly, "Hi. I'm Jackie," and I was both startled and encouraged by the fact that this fortune-teller appeared to be a typical suburban homemaker in every way. She invited me to take a seat at her kitchen table and offered me a glass of water. She then pulled out a deck of cards and explained that she could "read" them and they would reveal things about me, my life and my future.

As she began her reading, she immediately informed me that she knew two things about me: that I was romantically involved with a prominent businessman and that I was in serious legal trouble. She proceeded to tell me what she saw in the cards. "Something is going to change for you, Mary. Whatever your lawyers are telling you will happen is not going to happen at all." She went on to say that "a door would open" for me and I would be able to avoid prison altogether, or at least to avoid being there for very long. Her words were music to my ears—just exactly what I had been waiting and wanting to hear. When the card reading ended, Jackie gave me a cassette tape of everything she had said and I gave her one hundred dollars. *Well, she's cheaper than a lawyer,* I thought. *At least she's got good news. Those attorneys don't have anything positive to say.*

I left her house that afternoon more lighthearted than I had been in weeks, asking, *How could she have known all that? What else can she tell me?* I didn't understand, but because I had been told that her power was spiritual, I trusted Jackie and her insights. And I truly believed what she had told me— that everything would end in my favor when all of the legal hassle was finished.

Several months passed before I actually went to trial. During that time, I felt like a ping-pong ball being knocked back and forth across a net. On one side, my attorneys had nothing but grim reports every time I spoke with them. On the other side, I continued my visits with Jackie, often making spur-of-the-moment appointments with her immediately after hearing from my legal team. Time after time, she assured me that everything would turn out well for me.

Perhaps because my attorneys seemed so discouraged about my case, I continued to search desperately for a way out of my situation—just in case "the door" Jackie spoke of never opened. Dealing with the contradiction between Jackie and my legal team was more than I could bear. On top of that, I was terrified and exhausted. One of my attorneys had advised me to leave my house by 5:30 or 6:00 every morning and not to return until midnight because, he said, "You could be arrested at any moment."

The combination of such intense fear and confusion drove me to attempt the most radical means of escape I could think of—suicide. *Yes,* I reasoned, *that will end everything forever. Then Mike and my family won't have to go through this inevitable trial and the agony of seeing me go to prison.*

That was my answer.

Late one night, I went to the pharmacy, and the minute I walked in, I knew exactly what to do, which combination of tablets and capsules would accomplish my desired result. I reached for the medications required in my "prescription for death," planning to put the pills in my pocket and drive home to take them with a glass of wine. It would be simple and it would be fast.

As I reached for the first bottle, my hand began to tremble uncontrollably as it pushed against an invisible, impenetrable wall in front of the container I needed. I reached again and once more my hand began to shake, so much that I could not grasp the bottle as I struggled to break through the barrier I could not see. After repeated attempts and failures to pull the medicines off the shelves, I finally gave up and went home.

Good grief, I said silently, *I can't do anything right. I can't even kill myself!* Since I could not even manage a successful suicide, I had no choice but to face the dismal facts of my life: I had to stand trial, and if convicted, I would have to go to prison. During the months between the indictment and the trial, I spent hours and hours building my case with attorneys, poring over inventory records and a myriad of documents related to the charges against me.

Several times, a trial date was set and then canceled. Every postponement worked against me because the patients who could have testified on my behalf were dying quickly as they succumbed to the AIDS virus. *This is crazy!* I thought. *I can't go to trial when my witnesses are disappearing right before my very eyes! Will there be anyone left to stand up and speak for me?*

No. When the rap of the gavel finally signaled that the trial had begun one sizzling summer day in 1992, I was without a single patient from the pharmacy whom I knew well enough to call as a witness. I gulped the first time I saw the title of my case: *The United States of America v. Mary Elizabeth Forsythe.* That was exactly how I felt—like the full force of an entire nation and its vast government resources were levied against me. The only people on my side were my attorneys and Rachel and Leah, my co-defendants. Rachel and Leah testified about the cold, hard business facts of the pharmacy, but they certainly could not testify as character witnesses on my behalf. With indictments of their own, they were not exactly considered credible! I did have more than 400 letters from friends who supported me and wrote to the judge requesting mercy, but the court refused to admit those documents as evidence.

In the end, when all the arguments had been made, the evidence examined and the testimonies heard, the jury determined my destiny, at least for the foreseeable future: "Guilty on all counts." With that verdict nailed on me like a "Condemned" sign on a dilapidated old house, I had one goal for the days ahead—to find a way out of the trouble I was in.

Chapter 6

Shockwaves

The period of time between the trial's end in June and the sentencing in October was a flurry of activity. I lost myself in the process of closing the pharmacy and wondering what to do next. I could not resume the life I had been living, at least professionally, and I could not make plans for my future when my future was so uncertain.

The investigation had been grueling and the trial had been wrenching, but through it all, Mike was a rock for me, and no one was more intimately involved in my life than he was. He analyzed the trial in a hundred different ways and was well acquainted with my legal team. Because we could not ignore the prison term looming ahead of me, he joined me in feverish attempts to find a loophole or a strategy or some other way—*any* way—to keep me out of jail.

Surely we can find someone to help us, we thought as we placed urgent phone calls and wrote letters to about a dozen influential friends of our families. None of them could pull any strings or call in any favors to assist me, they said. My problems were too complicated and my trouble was too deep.

Even though we felt we did not have a second to spare from our efforts to ensure my freedom, we took time one afternoon to meet Mike's mother for tea at a Dallas hotel. We had not been seated long when his cell phone rang. As he spoke and listened, I watched the tension in his face ease and wondered what he was hearing.

After he hung up his phone, he reported that the caller was Mr. McWilliams, a local attorney who knew of Mike's family. Somehow, this man we'd never met had heard of my situation and wanted to talk with us. He had indicated to Mike that he might be able to help, so we left our still-steaming tea on the table, excused ourselves from Mike's mother and went immediately to Mr. McWilliams' downtown office with the first tiny burst of hope we had felt in several months.

Upon entering his office, hope turned into trust as my eyes landed on a framed photo of Judge John Faulk—the same Judge John Faulk who had presided over my trial. Mr. McWilliams noticed that my gaze was locked onto Judge Faulk's picture and explained that he and the judge were not only old friends, but that Judge Faulk had served as his legal intern many years earlier. From all appearances, I had just hit the jackpot. Mr. McWilliams seemed to have everything I needed—not only a personal friendship with Judge Faulk, but also a personal friendship with the President of the United States. With this unexpected boon, we realized that Mike's family had a network of connections that somehow reached all the way to the White House, and Mr. McWilliams was the missing link. Finally! My key to freedom—a presidential pardon.

We faced only one obstacle, really just a formality, according to Mr. McWilliams. Because my sentence had not yet been handed down, Mr. McWilliams could not do much for me immediately. As soon as I was sentenced, he said, he would begin the formal process of requesting the pardon. He assured us of his genuine willingness to help and instructed us to stay in touch with him.

Mike and I left Mr. McWilliams' office confident in his ability to help us and convinced that the pardon would indeed come through for me. We breathed a long, collective sigh of relief and went out to dinner to celebrate. Over a quiet meal and a bottle of wine at one of our favorite restaurants, we marveled at the connections between Mr. McWilliams, Judge Faulk and the president. Rejoicing in our good fortune, we began to dream again.

But we soon discovered that no one else interpreted our meeting with Mr. McWilliams as positively as we did. Our families and friends did not join our jubilee, but hesitated to believe that Mr. McWilliams and the President would actually be able to keep me out of prison. We dismissed their comments as naive and continued to throw the full weight of our trust onto Mr. McWilliams' promise.

The relief that accompanied our encouraging meeting with Mr. McWilliams did not last long—at least for me. Within several weeks, I found myself facing perhaps the only personal challenge powerful enough to pull my focus away from the gravity of my conviction.

I was pregnant.

What else can happen to me? I thought. I could hardly believe my life! After all I had personally experienced—and everything Mike and my family were going through—how could I possibly break this news to them? *What will Mike say?* I wondered. *Will he leave me? I can't lose him now!* I was already facing a prison term, and he had stood beside me so faithfully through some unusual and agonizing circumstances.

I assumed a baby would be more than he wanted to handle, so I knew what I had to do.

I dreaded telling Mike I was pregnant, but had already made up my mind to have an abortion by the time I informed him. At least I would be able to present him with a solution as soon as I mentioned the problem.

Over dinner that evening, I said to him, "Listen, I need to tell you something and it has nothing to do with my legal case." I took a deep breath and continued, "I'm pregnant. I want to have an abortion, and I need your help."

To my total shock, Mike whispered urgently, "No." His eyes filled with tears as he said again, "No, I don't want you to do that. This is my baby too."

I could see the wheels spinning in his mind for a moment before he spoke again, "We can make this work," he assured me. "I know what to do."

I braced myself, still astonished by his opposition to my very simple solution.

He began by saying, "Let's get married around the beginning of October," which was only a few weeks away.

Then, forcing himself, and me, to consider the possibility that I really could end up in prison, he continued, "If you have to go, I'll rent a house near the prison and hire a nanny to care for our child when I have to travel on business." Otherwise, he said, he was willing to function as a single parent until I was released.

He had everything worked out. "Once you've served your time," he assured me, "we'll get a house somewhere, put the past behind us and go on. We'll have a normal family life when this is all over."

I was stunned by his strategy. His loving response melted my heart, and I agreed to his plan.

One Monday morning not long after I had shared my unexpected news with Mike, and only five days before our wedding, I began to have some strange physical symptoms and called my friend and OB/GYN, Dr. Phyllis Gee. Following her instructions, Mike and I went immediately to her office for a sonogram, only to discover that I was suffering from an extremely rare condition called a blighted ovum, in which all the medical symptoms and confirmations of pregnancy were present—even a placenta and a sac—but no fetus. There was no baby!

Dr. Gee admitted me to the hospital that afternoon for an outpatient surgical procedure and then sent me home to "rest and recover" for several days. *I can rest all right*, I thought. *But I will need more than several days to recover from this latest traumatic event in my roller-coaster life.*

When Mike and I found out that we did not have to consider a baby, we decided to delay our wedding indefinitely even though all the plans were made, the dresses were bought, gifts had been sent and the honeymoon was arranged. Since Mike had already paid for our trip and we desperately needed some time away from the intensity of our everyday existence, we went. And while we were gone, my life would change drastically—again.

We spent a gorgeous and semi-relaxing week in northern California, hiking the grandeur of Yosemite Park, staying at an upscale health spa and driving in a convertible—top down—along the ruggedly beautiful Pacific coast. We spent the last night of our time away in Carmel, where Mike had made reservations at a luxury hotel. He decided after we checked into our room that he did not want to stay there. Tired and resisting a change of venue, I said to him, "This hotel is great. Why don't you want to stay here?"

"I don't know," he responded. "I just don't like it." Frustrated, I followed him to the car, and we drove away from our perfectly good accommodations.

We tried two other hotels, but both were full, and I was running out of patience by the time we drove into the parking lot of the third. The innkeeper there informed us that a convention was in town and all the local hotels were booked to capacity. "But," he said, "I have a friend who just built a guesthouse about a mile from here. I could call and see if it's available."

With neither question nor comment, Mike responded, "We'll take it."

The innkeeper gave us directions after calling his friend, and within minutes we arrived at a quaint little cottage where a woman was waiting outside for us. She greeted us with a smile and informed us that we were her first guests. I did not return her smile, nor pay attention to anything she said: my eyes were fixed on the baby she held in her arms. Surely I had seen other mothers with babies since my own bizarre experience, but for some reason, the sight of that mother and child took my breath away as I silently realized, *that could have been me.* Medically, I was never pregnant, but emotionally, I was. And I never knew how much it mattered, how deeply I had been touched by my own situation until I caught a glimpse of another woman's reality, a reality that was almost mine.

Noticing that something was bothering me, Mike drew his conversation with our hostess to a close and led me toward the guesthouse. As we turned to walk away, she stopped us and told us about a historic Carmelite Monastery just minutes away from her property and added, "You'd probably enjoy that." We agreed, and since the next day was Sunday, we decided to attend a service there.

We woke to a quiet, misty morning and headed toward the monastery after breakfast. We wound our way up a coastal highway and arrived to discover that it truly was a sight to see—a beautiful, seemingly ancient complex that was blanketed with peace and shrouded with a sense of history.

We made our way into the room where the service was held and enjoyed the music and the liturgy. When it came time to celebrate the Eucharist (or communion, as I called it), I was irresistibly drawn to the altar and found myself walking down the aisle, with Mike close behind. I joined the line to the altar not because I wanted to, but because I could not resist the inexplicable urge in my heart to go forward.

When the service concluded, the Mother Superior invited parishioners and visitors to share their prayer requests with her. A light suddenly switched on in both of our heads, and Mike and I looked at each other as if to say, "Prayer—what a novel idea!"

Mike approached Mother Frances and began to tell her our story. She slowly extended her hand toward me, and I responded by taking it in mine, as Mike continued to expound on our situation. The instant my hand touched hers, I felt as though I had been soaked in gasoline and lit with a match. A powerful current, like electricity, surged through my fingers, up my right arm, up my neck, to the top of my head. Like wildfire, the rush of pure power raced through my entire body. I began to weep uncontrollably and to shake as something thundered through me like another life force.

I was completely consumed—and completely confused. Because I had not cried a single tear throughout my whole ordeal, Mike thought I had finally broken emotionally in response to hearing him tell Mother Frances our story. If not that, he reasoned, maybe my display of emotion was the result of seeing a mother with her baby the previous day. But my tears were not provoked by any kind of feeling, nor were they born out of any natural circumstance.

Mike helped me to a nearby pew, where I continued trembling and sobbing for the next forty-five minutes. I could not possibly explain what was going on inside of me, so finally, a baffled Mike carried me to the car and we drove away from the monastery. Wanting to try to explain, I attempted to speak, but could not. I was literally struck dumb for three-and-a-half hours as waves of electricity continued to course through me.

That afternoon, when I was able to talk again, I remained unsure about exactly what had happened to me, so I asked Mike. After all, he was a seminary graduate and certainly knew more about spiritual experiences than I did. He could not explain it either. Instead of answering my questions, he launched into an explanation of the various orders of nuns in the Catholic church and tried to educate me about what kind of monastery we had visited. I couldn't have cared less. Mike's intellectual knowledge and his academic training could not help me, and because the incident was beyond our ability to comprehend mentally, we eventually just pretended that it never happened.

We left California that afternoon and flew back home, but the memory of my encounter at the monastery continued to live and breathe in my mind. Almost immediately after our return to Dallas, I called Mother Frances.

"Mother Frances, do you remember me? I'm the one who's going to prison. My fiancé and I asked for prayer the other day after we visited your church service."

"Of course I remember you," she said.

"Did you feel anything when you shook my hand?"

"No. I didn't feel anything."

Great. Even *she* could not explain it. *What am I going to do now?* I wondered. *Mike can't help me; even the Mother Superior can't help me!* I could have been tempted to doubt the whole experience or to decide I had suffered some sort of breakdown, but it was too real. I knew something incredible had occurred, but I would have to wait several months before I began to understand what happened to me in Carmel.

Chapter 7

Waiting

As soon as Mike and I arrived back in Dallas, the pressure of my situation quickly overwhelmed us because my sentencing hearing was scheduled within one week of our return. We would soon find out exactly how bleak my future would look.

In the midst of the tension, though, I could not keep from thinking about my brief meeting with Mother Frances and asking myself, *What in the world has happened to me?* If I did end up in prison, I wondered if maybe someone there could offer some insight. *Probably not,* I thought, doubting that anything very dramatic or spiritual could happen there.

On the day of my sentencing, I drove downtown to the Earl Campbell Federal Building, as I had done so many times. Dreading another court appearance, I ended up in the same courtroom where my trial had been held and my guilty verdict pronounced. Jeers and taunts and painful memories whispered from the walls as I waited for my turn to stand once again before Judge Faulk.

The sentencing, a process that would forever alter my life, only lasted about fifteen minutes. However, during that short time, to build a case for a lengthy prison stay, the prosecuting attorney did read one letter to the judge. Written just prior to death by an AIDS patient who suffered from dementia, it read, "Mary Forsythe is such an evil person she deserves to go to hell." In my opinion, hell had already pointed its best guns straight at me.

Judge Faulk pronounced a five-year sentence to be followed by three years of probation, tearing eight years of my life away from me in an instant. Because the Thanksgiving and Christmas holidays were just weeks away, my attorney asked the judge not to order me to prison until after the first of the new year. Judge Faulk agreed and set the date and time I was to self-surrender at the federal women's prison in Benton, Texas: January 5, 1993, at 1:00 P.M.

But I've got my whole life in front of me! I thought. And the judge had just informed me that some of my best years were going to be spent behind bars. I could not believe my ears. I realized that, up until that moment, prison had been purely theoretical to me. Reality's ugly finger had been wagging in my face for months, but I refused to see it until the instant Judge Faulk ordered me to a specific institution on a specific day at a specific time.

Even though I was stunned, I managed to remember two things. First, Jackie had assured me after a card reading that, even if I had to go to prison, something would happen and I would not have to stay long because a door would open for me. But I also had one more solid, practical hope that was still alive, my guaranteed escape route—the presidential pardon. *Then again,* I thought, *maybe the pardon* is *the door.*

As soon as my sentence was handed down, Mike and I contacted Mr. McWilliams and asked him to file the pardon request immediately. By late October 1992, after the paperwork had reached the White House, he received word, and a letter of confirmation, that the President had agreed to sign it. What a relief! Finally, things were working out for me the way they always had—a little adventure, a little drama and an uncanny ability to land on my feet.

I had promised my mother that everything would be all right the day I was found guilty in court. *She shouldn't have worried,* I thought. Being sentenced to prison was a close call, but thanks to the pending pardon, I was going to get out of trouble this time after all.

Mike and I were thrilled, and our confidence soared on the wings of the promise from Washington. The President had plenty of time to sign my pardon before I was supposed to report to prison in January, so we were not concerned. We stayed in close communication with Mr. McWilliams' office, and every time we questioned the status of the pardon, he assured us that everything was in order—the paperwork had been properly filed, and he was in touch with the authorities regularly. On top of that, he reminded us of the President's letter, in which he had agreed to sign the pardon papers. We just needed to be patient.

We were not accustomed to patience, but we had no choice. Waiting for a pardon was certainly better than waiting for a prison term! I reminded myself again of Jackie's door. I believed her just as much as I believed Mr. McWilliams, and between the two of them, I was convinced prison would not be a long-term engagement for me—if I had to go at all.

Faithful as ever, my parents drove to Texas to spend

Thanksgiving with Mike and me at his ranch. I was glad to see them, but the intensity of the uncertainty in our lives was almost unbearable. Nevertheless, Mike and I had decorated his house in preparation for their arrival—perhaps in an effort to make the holiday appear normal, when in fact, nothing was normal at all.

One of the things I always liked about my parents was their steadiness. They had always been the type who tried to duplicate their way of life at home wherever they were. And so, true to form, my dad quietly read the newspaper every morning, sitting in an easy chair, with a cup of black coffee in his right hand, while my mother substituted a brisk walk around the ranch for her typical morning golf game. Something about the dependability of their routine was comforting to me as it reminded me of the simpler, safer days of my life. But everything was different now; nothing was simple and I certainly was not safe.

On Thanksgiving Day, my sister joined us at the ranch, and Mike and I cooked a traditional dinner for my family. He even rented a horse and wagon for an old-fashioned hayride, but the false festivity we tried to create failed and the entire weekend was strained, awkward and generally miserable for everyone.

As my parents left to return to Kentucky, all of us knew that we had not really celebrated a holiday, but that we had at least been able to wait together and to hope together. And we did not know how much longer we would have that privilege.

December normally brought the happy confusion that came with gift buying and parties and all the activity of preparing for Christmas. As December 1992 began, it was full of confusion, but it was not happy. Every click of the "pardon clock" compounded our anxiety and chaos began to reign within me. One minute I was defiant, certain that my pardon would be granted. The next, I was silently fearful that it would not. My emotions bounced up and down like a rubber ball, my thoughts ran wild, and I darted in and out of denial like a racecar on a speedway. The frustration intensified until I thought I would either experience a spontaneous combustion or a total meltdown. I wanted the uncertainty to end, but I wanted it to end the "right" way—with me free to return to some semblance of a normal life, *not* with me locked in a jail cell in a federal prison.

By mid-December, when I had not heard anything definitive about my pardon, I began to wonder if something was wrong but clung to Mr. McWilliams' word and Jackie's promise. When I kept hearing "just be patient," from him and looking for a door I could never find, I sometimes gave up hope. At other times, I was able to convince myself that they were right. Through the ups and downs, I kept reminding myself that I just needed one simple scrawl, a presidential signature, on my pardon. Then I could proceed with my life.

Actually, I never stopped making plans to proceed with my life. Because I surrendered my pharmacist's license, as my attorney advised me after the trial, I knew that I could not practice pharmacy again, at least until all my legal troubles were behind me. But I was far too entrepreneurial, far too proactive, to sit around a ranch waiting to see what would happen to me. I needed something to do. I was brain-weary and emotionally exhausted from my ordeal and from the mysterious delay in the granting of my pardon. But I knew where to escape—to the one arena in which I had always been successful and had always been in control: the business world.

Throughout my friendship with Vincent and Katrina, we had discussed several joint ventures, but none had ever materialized. Before my trial, an opportunity had arisen for us to purchase a china factory in Hungary. Just what I needed—an international venture that would challenge me in a brand-new way. Obviously, my participation in the deal was put on hold during my legal battle, but the opportunity was still alive as I kept waiting for the news of my presidential pardon. Once it came through, I reasoned, I would devote my energies to the successful purchase of the china factory and to all the details of that transaction.

Judge Faulk had ordered me to pay a substantial sum of restitution to the United States government as part of my sentence. I had already sold my car and the government had started liquidating my assets in order to pay the money. But I expected the pardon to release me from any financial obligation beyond what the authorities had already collected and to free the money for my business pursuit. I felt better knowing that my plans for my immediate future were in place— and they did not include a prison term!

It was mid-December, so I would not have to wait long for the pardon to be granted. The President *had* to sign it before January 20, because a newly-elected President would take office that day.

My parents returned at Christmas time and that holiday was a sad re-run of Thanksgiving, except Mike and I had exchanged the colors in our fall decorations for red and green. We made more marvelous meals, played Christmas music and attended several traditional events, such as *The Nutcracker*. Once again, we did everything we could to make the holidays bright, all in one vain attempt after another to pretend— maybe even to believe—that nothing was wrong. We never convinced ourselves or anyone else.

We woke on Christmas morning with knots in our stomachs and lumps in our throats, but felt we had no choice except to contribute to simulated happiness as we exchanged gifts. Shopping had been emotionally difficult for everyone, yet we had all managed to have presents under the tree for each other. I knew Mike had bought me something special but had no idea what that gift might be. He handed me a small box, and after I had unwrapped it, I found a gold necklace with a small cross pendant. I tended to wear more ornate jewelry and was struck by the simplicity of the cross. Although I did not understand all of the meaning behind his gift, I could tell that he believed it was significant. As I looked at my pretty new necklace, I thought, *Well, we could certainly use some divine intervention about now!*

The Dallas Morning News routinely published the names of people who had been granted presidential pardons, so every morning during the holidays someone made the seemingly endless trip to the end of Mike's driveway and picked up the newspaper while the rest of us held our breath. While other families had looked forward to opening presents on Christmas Day, we were simply anxious to open the paper every morning. Nothing covered in shiny gift wrap and tied with a bow could have been a better present than finally seeing my name on the pardon list. Day after day we scoured the paper, expecting to see the one entry that would keep me at home and out of prison. And day after day, we saw scores of other names, but never mine.

But as the old saying goes, "Hope springs eternal," and on many occasions, I pulled the newspaper out of the trash can and carefully re-read the pardon lists, honestly believing it was possible that four literate adults had actually missed the one entry we were looking for.

As my parents loaded their car and prepared to leave, I overheard my mother say to my dad, "What's going to happen to our Mary?" Dad and I both knew she did not want to hear the answer to her question. She simply needed to ask.

Mike was also concerned about what would happen to me and began to make some practical preparations, *just in case*. He thoroughly investigated the facility at Benton as much as possible from a distance—the physical size of the prison, the number of inmates incarcerated there, who the warden was and what personal items I would be allowed to take with me.

He also contacted Prison Fellowship, a Christian prison ministry, and they arranged for an inmate from Benton, named Gloria, to correspond with me prior to my arrival. Although I received several letters from her and spoke with her once by phone, I did not think Mike's efforts to stay in touch with her were necessary and did not take our communication as seriously as I should have. *Why should I?* I thought, *Even if I do have to go, it won't be for long.* I knew that presidents often signed pardons as one of their last official acts. Since my surrender date was January 5 and the President would leave office on January 20, I finally resigned myself to the fact that I might have to spend up to fifteen days behind bars.

It'll be all right, I convinced myself. I had lived a most interesting life and could simply add a visit to prison to my list of adventures. It would be hard—and terribly inconvenient—but after everything I had endured through the investigation and the trial, I could do anything for about two weeks—even prison.

Chapter 8

Day One

I had never packed for a trip like this before. Then again, I had never been to a place like prison before. I had prepared for plenty of two-week trips in my life, but knew that this time away from home would not require a swimsuit, evening clothes or a change of purses.

I remembered Gloria's letters and phone call. She had tried to introduce me to prison life—a world of its own, totally foreign to anything I had ever encountered. She attempted to make my transition as smooth as possible by giving me specific information on how many civilian clothes I could take with me, what kinds of personal items I could have and what to expect during the check-in process at Benton.

Based on her information, I placed my few permitted belongings into my small suitcase. With part of me aware that I had to go to prison first thing the next morning, and part of me hiding away in my familiar den of denial, I never once thought about the fact that the bag I was packing in the privacy of my own luxurious bedroom would be unpacked by total strangers in a harsh and dismal place and in a grossly impersonal way. It was a good thing I did not know what really awaited me as I made final preparations to leave Dallas.

After a few restless hours of sleep, I awakened at 4:00 A.M. to my last morning in my own home. Mike and I were scheduled to leave Dallas at 5:00, and just before we walked out of my house, he handed me a package. As a going-away gift, or more as an "I-really-love-you; wear-this-and-remember-me" gift, he presented me with a thick terry cloth bathrobe on which each sleeve, pocket and panel was a different color. He called it my "coat of many colors" because it made him think of the Bible story about Joseph and the brightly-colored cloak his father gave him. I did not know anything about this Joseph, but I loved the robe and hoped the prison officials would not take it away.

Riding in the passenger seat of Mike's car as we drove away from my home and everything familiar to me, I clung to the last-minute hope that the presidential pardon would come through sometime while we were on the highway between Dallas and Benton. We arrived in the town of Benton at 11:00 A.M., and I did not have to report to prison until 1:00 that afternoon. We made a final, frantic phone call to Mr. McWilliams, desperate to hear that my promised pardon had been granted. He had heard nothing, he said. Washington was silent. And those last two hours before I had to report to prison were like a deathwatch.

With our last hope extinguished, Mike and I walked around a nearby mall, just to pass the time and to try to avoid really facing the heartbreak that ravaged both of us. We purchased some make-up and a few toiletries because, by that time, one thing was undeniably clear: I was indeed going to prison.

At 12:30 P.M., we drove through the gates of the federal women's prison. I could hardly believe I was *early* for prison. Mike dropped me off at the Receiving and Discharge building (which the inmates called "R and D") and, as he helped me out of the car, the guards ordered him to leave the grounds immediately. In a poor attempt to hide my fear behind an exhortation, I said to him, "Be sure the car is clean when you come to get me in two weeks!" I was trying to be strong, though I was terrified inside—trying to hold myself together for him—and for me.

Then he was gone. I was on my own—alone, afraid, exhausted—embarking on a strange course that would take me places I never dreamed I'd go.

As much as Gloria tried to help, nothing—absolutely nothing—could have made me ready for what I actually experienced. A federal women's prison is not a sorority house. There are no books or instructional tapes, no video interviews with inmates that can truly prepare a person for the sudden and complete loss of freedom that takes place when she crosses the line between ordinary citizen and federal prisoner. But more than that, there is no way to adequately warn a person of the emotional tidal wave that hits when her identity is jerked away.

The check-in process was grueling. As I entered the R and D center, I saw two other women who were also being checked in. I was astonished by how rough and how frightening they looked; and I was horrified that the three of us were on a common journey. The prison authorities could force me to go through the same motions as the other two women, I decided, but they could not make me see myself as "one of them." To all appearances, the other women and I could not have possibly been more different. I certainly did not have any patience for them as I quickly assessed their clothes, hairstyles and lack of personal hygiene and passed judgment on them with a loud, proud, disgusted sigh.

I was tired and frustrated as I began the transformation from a name to a number, from a person to a prisoner. The first phase of the check-in process elicited an emotional response that caught me by surprise. I was shocked and embarrassed as prison guards rummaged through my suitcase, scrutinizing each piece of clothing, even inspecting the seams of my undergarments to make sure I had not tried to sneak in any contraband. They examined each of my personal items and separated them into two piles: what I could keep and what I could not.

When they finished, the "what-you-can-keep" pile was tiny. I was devastated as they took away most of the things Mike and I had bought at the mall less than two hours earlier. Tossing those items in a box, they asked me, "Where do you want this shipped?" Even though I knew receiving that package would break Mike's heart, I gave them his name and address, hoping he would understand and wishing the officers would just let me include a short note of explanation. Already, after only being in prison a short while, I knew better than to ask.

Gloria had been honestly mistaken about what items I could take in with me, and I was not allowed to have nearly as much as she thought. Policies and rules changed at random in prison, and they had changed between the time she spoke with me and the time I arrived in Benton. She, of course, was never informed of the changes, and I later realized that experience was my first indication of some of prison's most frustrating characteristics: arbitrary decisions, little or no communication and an unusual tolerance for chaos.

As I completed the check-in process, the playing field was leveled. For so long, my possessions had defined my identity. Then suddenly, I had no more than anyone else, and every inch of what I did have had been thoroughly examined by total strangers. I could tell that I would not be able to impress anyone in Benton. I had always used my cars or my house or my clothes or my credit cards when I wanted to make an impact, but those things were out of my reach now. It was only my first day, and the prison officials had knocked out from under me a pedestal that took years to build!

They did allow me to keep my new robe, which was nicer than anything any other inmate possessed. But even with my superior bathrobe, for the first time in my life, all things were equal. The only thing I had more of than anyone else was my arrogance.

An officer escorted me to a holding tank and put me in it with the other two women who had self-surrendered that day. One wall of the holding tank was glass and the other three were made of cinder blocks painted a stark, flat, lifeless shade of white. The small room felt no warmer than 40 degrees and it contained one stainless steel toilet—one *cold* stainless steel toilet—located where everyone inside and outside the tank could see it. An eerie mixture of dread and disgust rose up in me as we entered the cell. Then I heard a sound that jolted me out of any remaining denial—the thud of a door slamming behind me and the hollow clang of a large lock. It was a door to which I did not have a key, a door I could not open. My freedom had vanished.

Standing, shivering in the holding tank, I finally began to realize that this experience was not simply the next and most dramatic installment of my life's adventures, but that I really was a prisoner, a "common criminal" in the eyes of the world.

The other women and I stayed in the tank for several hours as I wrestled silently with the maddening uncertainty of what was yet to come. We exchanged the most basic information about ourselves, but avoided the subject of why we were there and how long we expected to stay. Our strained, shallow conversation did nothing to relieve my unsettled feeling that the worst still lay ahead of me.

I was accustomed to a fast-paced life and did not like sitting still, having time to wonder what was going to happen next. I liked to think quickly and move quickly and get things done quickly. I was a paragon of multi-tasking and efficiency, and so far nothing moved very fast in prison. In my mind, I streamlined the check-in process a multitude of ways and knew that what should have taken thirty minutes had already taken several hours. I was getting my first taste of the bureaucratic quagmire known as the Federal Prison Camp at Benton.

Another chip of denial fell off of me as I realized that even my time did not belong to me anymore. Everything, down to the smallest detail of my life, was now under someone else's control; I was no longer my own boss. This strong, independent woman was going to have to do things differently for a while, and that did not appeal to me in the least.

Finally, a guard unlocked the door of the tank and said, "Forsythe, get out here!" I could not remember ever being summoned in such a harsh, empty tone of voice, or being called only by my last name. "What's your number?" she asked.

"What number?" I responded, "My social security number?"

"No," she snapped, "your *number*." Oh, right—the inmate I.D. number I had been issued. I couldn't remember, so I fumbled through pockets until I found my I.D. card and awkwardly read the eight-digit number to her.

My metamorphosis was complete. I had become just another inmate, just another federal offender who got caught and sent to this inefficient place to be punished. I was no longer "Mary," but "22490-077." I could hear the "plop" as another piece of my identity hit the floor. As the guard led me around a corner into an area where the prison uniforms were stored, she told me to memorize that number and to keep my inmate I.D. card with me at all times. *This is getting tougher by the minute,* I said to myself.

The uniforms were kept on wide gray metal shelves, with all the shirts crammed into one set of shelves and all the pants stuffed in another. A third section of shelves housed a heap of wadded socks, with the underwear next to them. I was struck by how monochromatic everything was—and how ugly!

Listening to the guard rehearse instructions she muttered every day, I tried to remember what she said. Was it three pairs of pants and two shirts, or two pairs of pants and three shirts? *Oh well,* I thought, *she won't hesitate to correct me if I don't get it right.* I picked through the jumbled piles of khaki canvas shirts and pants only to discover that everything had been previously worn and that nothing was too clean. I chose some clothes that looked as though they would fit and was issued two pair of shoes—some heavy, black steel-toed work boots and a pair of brown shoes. I also received several pairs of used athletic socks, several thin green T-shirts and some institutional underwear—at least that was brand new. Not much of a wardrobe.

With my prison uniforms in hand, I suspected that I would soon have to change out of my civilian clothes and into the "new" clothes I had been issued—and I knew what that meant.

I dreaded the strip search more than anything and had even asked Gloria about it. She had responded only that it would not take long and that I would survive it. It had been delayed so far, but no longer. It was time for the last piece of my dignity to be taken away.

An officer directed me behind a curtain, where my worst fears were given credence. I had hoped against hope that I would be able to change clothes without having to suffer this intimate and humiliating inspection. Everything in me was terrified and enraged and plummeting to new depths of shame all at the same time.

No doubt, the guard who conducted the strip search had robbed the privacy and self-respect of dozens, maybe even hundreds, of inmates before me, but this was *my* first time. On the outside I stood silently still, feeling the chill of the cool, stale prison air against my bare skin, but blazing inside with the heat of mortal embarrassment. Having every inch of my body patted and prodded and closely inspected broke whatever strength might have remained in me. Like the rape years before, that experience, too, stole something from who I was and killed something deep within me.

I did survive the wretched strip search that terrible day and countless days afterward. Though each time brought a fresh and piercing sense of violation, nothing could ever compare to that first time. I understood why Gloria had not been able to share much. It was just too horrible to talk about.

When it was over, I dressed in my prison uniform, and the officer ordered me to put my civilian clothes into a brown paper bag with my greatly-reduced collection of personal items. A guard then took me to another holding tank to wait for the two other women who were checking in with me. I could not speak for them, but what I had been through had resulted in not only a different set of clothes, but a different woman. When they arrived, we were all dressed alike and we had all systematically lost elements of our identity as the afternoon progressed. Piece by piece, our freedom had been whittled away to the point that we had no liberty left at all.

The prison required a medical examination, which I did not want to endure. I volunteered no information and answered all questions as quickly and succinctly as possible. I was concerned because, several months earlier, I had been diagnosed with a tumor on a bone in my right foot. I had planned to have it treated, but did not take the time after I became engrossed in my legal case and the trial. *This is just great,* I thought sarcastically, *here I am in prison with a tumor.* Even so, I knew enough about medical care in government institutions to know that I did not want to be treated in one. I told no one about the growth on my foot. I had endured it for several months already and, though it did cause pain, I knew I could certainly live with it for another fifteen days. I made a mental note to see the doctor when I returned to Dallas.

As the guard escorted my two new acquaintances and me out of the R and D building, I got my first glance at the prison yard. As I walked down the narrow sidewalk, carrying my bedroll (which consisted of a thin, gray blanket, a sheet and a pillow) and my small sack of belongings, I could sense hundreds of eyes glaring at me. I later learned that when new inmates arrived, the entire prison population took notice and peered out the windows more out of defiance than curiosity because no one wanted additional cellmates.

We passed a small walking track and a pavilion before entering the courtyard of the four dormitories that housed more than 800 inmates and stopped outside of a dorm called

Jackson 1. The guard informed me that I had been assigned there, to a cell with two other inmates—reputedly the loudest, toughest women in the whole dorm.

My cramped first-floor cell contained two sets of bunk beds, four industrial-grade lockers, a tiny table and a plastic chair. The bathroom was located several cells down the hall from mine and serviced about fifty women. Everything was so sparse, so harsh-looking. I knew it was prison; I knew it was designed for punishment and not for comfort, but still, *I* never anticipated living in conditions like these.

But the physical environment was not nearly as challenging as my cellmates were. I had never known people like these women before. The guard was right: they were loud and they were tough, very tough. They seemed to be in conspiracy against me as they immediately tried to intimidate me with prison rules that turned out to be untrue. After they made sure I knew the "rules," they took turns gloating over the crimes they had been convicted of and wanting to know all about my case.

I just wanted to be left alone.

My cell did have one small window, from which I could see a rosebush. Even though it was January, two tiny blossoms clung to the branches. They were fading and fragile, but as I looked at them, I thought, *I bet I'll be gone before that last rosebud falls.* Watching those rosebuds became a game to me, an unofficial race to see who would stay longer where— they on the bush or me in prison.

Chapter 9

A Change of Plans

Prison was a long way from my upscale Highland Park lifestyle in more ways than one. Everything about my former existence screeched to an abrupt halt the instant I walked through the doors at Benton. The adjustment from my busy, comfortable life to the drudgery of prison was wrenching. On top of the seemingly contagious depression and low-grade bedlam that were almost tangible behind bars, the sudden and drastic loss of control—and the uncertainty that accompanied it—grated on me constantly. I was frightened and frazzled from all the events of the past months and years— but worse than that, I was at a total stand-still, completely powerless over my circumstances.

I could only find one dubiously good thing about the entire prison experience so far: the reflective quality of the bathroom mirrors was not much better than aluminum foil. My self-image was so terrible that I felt a strange sense of relief when I looked in them. After living with mirrors covering my bathroom walls at home and turning off the lights every time I walked by them, I was actually glad I could not see myself clearly. I hated myself that deeply.

But I could tell that prison was no place to recover from a bad self-image. *Maybe I'll try to do something about that when I get back home to Dallas,* I thought. Something about being in prison and unable to attend to things like the tumor in my foot and my long-time struggle with rejection spurred me to the realization that I needed to prioritize taking care of myself both physically and emotionally. Yes, I would deal with those issues when I got out. Even though I would be going home in a couple of weeks, I determined for the present moment to put aside my personal problems and concentrate on ways to survive my short stay behind bars without letting the monotony of prison overtake me.

Because Benton was a work prison, every inmate who was medically able was required to work, which meant having to report to the guard or officer who oversaw each particular job assignment. I was not accustomed to having to answer to anyone, but rather to having employees report to me. Nevertheless, I had no choice. I *had* to work; I *had* to have a boss; and I *had* to comply with whatever schedule the prison demanded.

Within the first few days of my incarceration, I began to find out about all the different places to work and discovered that the inmates practically kept the place running. Among other assignments, they worked in the kitchen, in the horticulture department, on construction teams, in the electrical and plumbing facilities and in the warehouse. Even though my pardon would soon be granted and I would be far away from prison, I was eager for any job other than the one I was given when I arrived.

For my first several days, I was "unassigned," which meant that I could be (and was) called upon to perform any duty, at any time, by any officer. Being unassigned was harder than many other jobs because it often meant being awakened around 5:00 A.M. by a guard shaking my bunk and screaming, "Get up!" I would then be ordered out into a bitterly cold, still-dark morning to sweep sidewalks with a heavy industrial broom and to pick up cigarette butts around the prison grounds.

Being unassigned was extremely difficult for me mentally because the jobs were so unpredictable and so unpleasant, which constantly reminded me that my entire life was under someone else's control. I hated not knowing where I was going, when I was to be there and what I was expected to do. I could not tolerate the uncertainty of being unassigned, and I could not unwind at the end of the day with a glass of wine. Besides that, I had no one to talk to. I seemed to have nothing in common with anyone, so I kept to myself as much as possible with the exception of a few conversations with Gloria.

Gloria had one of three coveted office jobs in the prison warehouse and suggested that I apply to work there too. Given my options, it seemed like a good choice, so I took her advice and my job request was soon granted. Relieved to finally have an assignment and to know where I would be going every weekday morning, I thought, *Well, at least this job will give me a routine and help make my short stay more bearable.*

The warehouse was located in the back of the prison yard, a three- or four-minute walk from my cell. A total of five inmates worked there, three in the office and two in the storage and receiving area, which housed all of the food and other supplies for the entire prison. I was assigned to manual labor. I had always been strong physically but had primarily used my mind in my work. Now, I would be forced to use my body and to push it beyond any limits it had ever known—hauling and lifting boxes and heavy bags of food for all of the inmates.

The hours at the warehouse were 7:30 A.M. until 3:30 P.M., with a lunch break from 11:30 until 12:15. I was required to wear my prison uniform and the black clunky, steel-toed work boots I had been issued. For my efforts, I would be paid seventeen cents per hour. I could have earned up to fifty cents per hour—almost three times what I made at the warehouse—but could not bear the thought of working at some of the higher-paying jobs. Most of them required long periods of time working with other inmates and constant exposure to their foul language, bad tempers and all sorts of other offensive behaviors. Because it did not take me long to realize how rare and precious even the tiniest bit of privacy was, I wanted to work in the warehouse. That job demanded less contact with large groups of raucous women than any other available assignment.

I had always considered manual labor somehow "beneath" me. After all, I was an educated woman, a professional. I reported to work my first day at the warehouse, lumbering awkwardly in my steel-toed work boots and clothed in a well-crafted air of superiority to hide my utter humiliation. I met the boss, Mr. Isaacs, who had clearly perfected the art of barking orders and reminded me of stories I had heard about drill sergeants.

I had a lot to learn about warehouse work. I knew how to handle filling prescriptions and counseling patients, but I knew nothing about unloading trucks with a dolly, transporting seventy-pound bags of food on my back and operating two kinds of forklifts. My job description from Mr. Isaacs also included mopping, painting, gathering and hauling trash, scrubbing stairs, cleaning out walk-in refrigerators, watering plants, cleaning restrooms and a host of other chores. By far, the worst thing Mr. Isaacs required me to do was to bait rattraps in the afternoons and check them the following morning to see, as he said, "if we got a catch." If this were not enough, when we did have a catch, Mr. Isaacs expected me to report back to him each victim's weight. I only had one thought, *This is sick.*

Once a week, my co-worker and I had to climb the stairs into a loft area where the office supplies were stored and fill supply requests for the other departments of the prison. For the first few weeks, that was one of my less objectionable duties, but like everything else, it quickly became mundane.

I had not been working in the warehouse long before I discovered that Mr. Isaacs not only gave the orders, but wanted them carried out according to his specific, rarely logical, instructions. A surge of pride and rebellion coursed through me when I discovered that I could not simply do my job, but that I had to do it *the way* Mr. Isaacs demanded. I could not just mop the floor, but had to move the mop in the awkward, unnatural circular motion he demonstrated—and while he watched. He had little patience as he observed my clumsy technique, and I had little patience for his domineering personality. Furthermore, when I used the forklift, I could not just operate it; I had to do it exactly the way he said to do it. *Driving this forklift the way he says to is driving me crazy!* I thought.

I did not like to be told what to do. I had forgotten what it was like to have to ask permission for *anything*, and in prison I had to ask permission for *everything*. There was no grace period, no leniency, no slap on the hand. I had not had to obey anyone for years and was accustomed to being my own boss—and that was the way I liked it. But in prison, I had absolutely no choice. I *had* to obey Mr. Isaacs, even though I did not respect him. The only acceptable response to him was, "Yes, sir."

Even as my mouth agreed to do things his way, my mind objected constantly: *I know a better way.* I discovered that despite the fact that all inmates wore the same type of drab uniform, the same kind of flimsy flip-flops to the shower and the same sort of institutional underwear, I still had my own unique brand of arrogance and rebellion. The prison officials could make me look like everyone else on the outside, but they could not touch me on the inside. They could enforce all sorts of rules and regulations on my behavior, but they could not prohibit my pride. I maintained my haughty attitude, doing precisely as Mr. Isaacs instructed, but silently criticizing him and resenting his authority.

It's only for two weeks, I kept reminding myself. Inauguration Day was drawing near, and with it, my promised pardon and release. I would be going home—back to Mike, back to some sort of busy, glamorous life in Dallas, back to a comfortable home and to clothes that were more than one color. I knew that the trial and everything surrounding it had certainly smudged my reputation; I also knew the scandal would subside. And of course, Mike was standing with me, and together we would be just fine. I simply had to keep from falling apart for a few more days.

I used the few sheets of stationery I was allowed to bring into Benton as a journal—a brief daily commentary on my life behind bars—and on January 12, 1993, I wrote:

1/12/93: I am watching one pink rose outside my window. There is peace even though one rose has fallen. The other is in its last days.

Nevertheless, I was still confident that I would win my

game with the rosebuds. The competition was stiffer with only one bud left, but competition always fueled me and I welcomed the new tightness of the race. It would only make my victory sweeter.

On January 16, four days before the Inauguration. I declared in my journal:

1/16/93: No matter what the news, I'll be fine. I'm strong; I can handle it.

On the afternoon of Wednesday, January 20, 1993, Mr. Isaacs reluctantly granted me permission to leave the warehouse to return to my dorm and make a collect phone call—the call that would put an end to my life as a federal prisoner. Finally, it was Inauguration Day! I knew that the President would have signed a number of pardons on his way out of office—and mine was in the stack.

Eager to hear the good news and ready to go home, I called Mike to find out when he would arrive to take me back to Dallas. The instant he answered the phone, I knew something was terribly wrong. He wept as he told me that there had been some kind of bureaucratic mistake and the pardon had not been signed. For some reason that no one could explain, he said, the papers never made it to the President's desk. I froze. For what seemed like an eternity, all I could hear on the other end of the line was the sound of tears hitting the mouthpiece of his phone.

For almost a year, Mike and I had tried zealously to keep me out of prison. We had focused our best efforts on that one goal, spending long hours and huge sums of money to avoid what had just happened. I was in prison to stay.

With a deep breath and a mediocre attempt to garner enough strength to speak through my shock, I responded,

"OK. What do we do next?" After we talked for a few minutes, I instructed Mike to begin the appeal process immediately. That would work. Yes. My attorney would file an appeal and everyone would see that I did not need to be in prison after all. We could have filed an appeal at any time after my trial but did not because we were so certain the pardon would be signed and that no further legal action would be necessary. I was sorry we had not started sooner. I knew that the appeal process could take up to a year, which meant I could spend another twelve months in prison, but at least I would not have to serve my full sentence. Stunned and struggling to hold my chin up, I headed back to the warehouse.

Determined not to let my devastation show, I went straight to the loft to avoid questions from other inmates in the warehouse and to think through what had just happened. The loft was farther away from people than anywhere else I was allowed to go, so I sought refuge and a measure of privacy there. Gloria saw me return and found me. She knew I was expecting a good word from Washington that day and asked what had happened. In an attempt to camouflage my pain with sarcasm, I replied, "I guess I should have bought a bigger tube of toothpaste." She had seen this particular disappointment before and was genuinely sympathetic. She told me, "This is a time to praise God. He has a plan for you, Mary. He has a plan you're totally unaware of—and His plan is good." I could not believe my ears.

How can she see this terrible news through spiritual eyes? I wondered. Her perspective took me by surprise. I had certainly "prayed" for my release—to the extent that I knew how to pray. I had also found that my increasingly desperate circumstances had begun to give birth to thoughts about God and to a longing to believe that He was involved in my everyday existence. Even so, I could not imagine how Gloria thought I could be thankful and praise God in the face of this unbelievable news. I finally decided that she just did not understand. But at the same time, I wondered if she might be right. Maybe there really was a whole realm, a whole way of looking at life, that I was not even considering. I thanked her and permitted her to give me a quick hug before she returned to her work in the office.

I allowed a trail of tears to wind down my face.

At the beginning of my incarceration, I had made a decision about getting emotional in prison—a personal pledge to not break down—because I was afraid I might never recover. I made that decision when I expected to be in prison no more than fifteen days. Now that I would be there longer, I made a fresh commitment to not let my feelings show. I strengthened my determination to "keep it together," even though I had just experienced one of the most devastating disappointments of my life. I rounded up all of my resolve, wiped the tears that had escaped from my eyes and got back to work.

That night, I remembered Gloria's words—that God had a plan—and wrote in my journal:

1/20/93: No good news from man. It is just not my time. Mr. McWilliams heard from Washington last night that the pardon was blocked—too many hurdles. I held on until noon. I didn't break until I got back to the warehouse. Gloria came up and I was okay at first. She gave me a hug and then I lost it. I said that I knew I should have bought a bigger tube of toothpaste. At least we smiled. She said it's time to praise God. Not my timing, but His.

Chapter 10

The Turning Point

I had not had a good week. The Saturday morning after Inauguration Day, I lay in my bunk, relieved that I did not have to go to work and still trying to absorb the shock of not being pardoned. I just wanted to go home.

1/23/93: Pink rose is turning brown. Only a few precious petals remain.

I was crushed, totally defeated in every way. Even the silly little imaginary game I had played with the rosebuds was almost over, and I was going to lose to a flower! *What am I going to do now?* I wondered. I had counted on a man's promise and the promise had failed. Who could I trust and where could I turn? I felt a heaviness in my heart that I had never felt before. The arrogant, independent woman who had walked into Benton a few weeks earlier assured of a presidential pardon had become confused, desperate and terribly frightened.

I rolled out of my prison bunk and onto my knees. I knelt on the cold, hard tile floor with my head in my hands and tears streaming down my face—I could not help it. I cried out with unprecedented brokenness in my heart, "God! *I* can't do it anymore! Help me!"

To my surprise, I heard a gentle voice whisper, "Mary, I have been waiting to hear you say that." In that moment, something happened deep within me. The heaviness lifted and the confusion and fear and pressure rolled off. In that instant, everything changed. The warden did not appear in my cell and announce, "Mary, you can go home now." Nothing in my external circumstances was different at all, but everything inside of me changed radically.

He had heard me! God had heard my cry—and He responded. The experience was so real, so personal and so deep in my heart that I was immediately convinced He would indeed help me. Somehow, I could sense His wholehearted commitment to me and somehow, I *knew* I could trust Him.

The next day, I attended a church service in the prison chapel. As we sang the profound and simple old song, "Jesus Loves Me," tears began streaming down my face—again. How many times had I sung that song as a child? More than I could count. In fact, I could not remember *not* knowing its familiar words, but it had never affected me at all. It certainly had not ever moved me to tears!

Why that time? I didn't know, but I cried tears I could not control. They were not emotional; they came from a tender place inside of me—a place that had never been touched before. I wrote in my journal that night:

1/24/93: Service was good. When we sang, "Jesus Loves Me," I cried.

Were my Sunday tears part of God's answer to my Saturday cry for help? Did "Jesus Loves Me" have something to do with my prayer? I could not answer those questions. I only knew that my hard heart had been softened and that somehow my tears were related to God. In ways I did not understand and could never explain, I *knew* He was helping me.

Stuck in prison, I was desperate enough to allow God to do anything He wanted. Facing the possibility of several years behind bars, and even after being at Benton just a few weeks, I was convinced I could not survive there on my own. I *had* to have help, and with family and friends and Mike a world away, God was all I had left. Even though I had sincerely asked for His help and believed He would send it, I was still shocked by what He did next.

Several Sundays later, I was once again sitting in a chapel service, not expecting any visitors that afternoon. An officer interrupted the service by saying, "Forsythe, you've got a visitor." I had forgotten to take my I.D. card with me, and it was necessary in order for me to be permitted to see a visitor. Thrilled because I thought Mike had come to surprise me and anxious because visiting hours were almost over, I race-walked back to my cell (running was against the rules), grabbed my I.D. and headed for the visiting room. By the time I arrived, only about fifteen minutes of visitation remained.

But when I looked around, Mike was nowhere in sight. I did not recognize anyone in the room! Mike, my sister and my mother and dad were the only four people on my approved visitors' list, and none of them was there. *This must be a mistake,* I thought. *I don't know anyone here.* Then a man I had never seen before walked up to me and asked, "Are you Mary?"

Annoyed by the nerve of this total stranger and wondering how he managed to be admitted to see me, I snapped,

"Yeah." I gave him my best condescending look and continued, my words dripping with sarcasm, "and who-o-o-o are you?"

"My name is Gary. And God sent me."

Those words caught my attention and replaced my arrogance with profound curiosity. Questions raced through my mind: *Who is this man? God sent him to see me? No way!* Something was highly unusual about the situation because my list of approved visitors did not include names of people I'd never met, and it really was humanly impossible for him to have been permitted to see me.

"Can we go outside and talk?" he asked.

After his announcement that God had sent him and the fact that someone in authority had allowed him to see me, I did not even consider saying anything but, "Yes."

We walked out into the small, fenced visiting yard where other inmates were talking with families and friends. It was a sunny Sunday afternoon and the outdoor visiting area was crowded, but we found a lone vacant bench under an oak tree near the back corner of the yard. Though no place in the visiting area was private and everyone there was subject to the watchful eyes and listening ears of the guards who monitored the inmates' every move, this bench was the most secluded spot that existed, and I wondered why it was unoccupied.

After we were seated, Gary looked at me with eyes that seemed to see all the way through me. Then he asked me the question that would change my life forever: "Do you want to receive the baptism of the Holy Spirit?"

In all the years I spent going to church, I never heard of "the baptism of the Holy Spirit." However, several days earlier, I had stumbled across a small booklet on top of a trashcan.

When I picked it up and flipped it open, I saw these words: "When you don't know how to pray, pray in the Holy Spirit." I thought, *I need that because I really don't know how to pray.* But I quickly dismissed that notion and tossed the book into the trashcan. I had no idea what "pray in the Holy Spirit" meant and was not hopeful that anyone at Benton could tell me.

But somehow, when Gary asked me if I wanted to receive the baptism of the Holy Spirit, I *knew* he was talking about the same thing that was in the little booklet I had thrown away. I reminded myself that I had asked God to help me and believed He would. Was it possible that the God who had sent Gary to me was also speaking to him about me— right that very minute? I had to know. With one finger pointing toward heaven, I said, "Did He ask you to ask me that?"

"Yes. He did."

So I responded, "Then yeah. I do."

Gary said, "Stand up."

He stood about two feet from me and, without a word, extended his hand and barely touched my forehead with his index finger. Down I went. I fell to the ground and lay on my back as though the undercurrent of an ocean had swept my feet from beneath me.

I had no frame of reference for what was happening to me. I had never seen, much less experienced, anything like this before—not in the movies, not on television and certainly not in real life. It was not even the same kind of experience I had at the monastery in Carmel. Although I did not understand what was going on, it was not scary; it was not violent; and it was not painful. It was gentle, loving, peaceful—and it was filled with grace. I later came to understand that in that instant, the power of the Holy Spirit had overwhelmed me to the point that I was unable to stand.

Gary knelt beside me, put his hands on my stomach and began to pray. At least I assumed he was praying, but his words were not in English. I thought, *Wow. This guy is bilingual.* I was impressed by his fluency and wondered what language he was speaking. Didn't he know I could not understand him? Why did he find it necessary to speak a foreign language in the middle of a prison yard with me lying on the ground? I quickly reviewed the languages I heard when I traveled in Europe years earlier. His words did not sound French or Italian or Spanish or German, which only increased my intrigue because he was conversant in a language so unlike any I had ever heard.

Still lying on the ground with my eyes closed, I heard an unusual sound—a storm roaring toward us like a freight train barreling down the track. I heard the wind whipping, the leaves of the oak tree rustling and could tell that the branches were shaking. *If he doesn't hurry up,* I thought, *we're going to get wet.*

But there was no storm; the afternoon remained perfectly clear and still. The storm was actually brewing in a realm I could not see, but I could hear it as though it were just inches away. I had encountered some strange things in my life, but this experience was the most bizarre yet. It made absolutely no sense to my mind, but I felt I had gone too far to turn back.

At that moment, my tongue began to slide backwards in my mouth as if something were pulling it through the back of my neck. *What on earth is happening to me?* I wondered. I could hardly breathe, and then I began to gag and choke. Immediately, Gary switched from his unknown language back to English, and said, with great composure yet with great authority, "In the name of Jesus, come out of her." I could not explain what happened in that instant except to say that something evil left me, and something wonderful filled me.

What I thought was a foreign language was actually a heavenly language. Gary had been praying in tongues, the language of the Holy Spirit. God granted me the ability to perceive the storm I heard raging in the invisible realm, to peer into that realm and glimpse just one scene of the spiritual battle for my life—a conflict between God and the devil—a war that had lasted, and would last, all of my life. The conflict exploded around and within me because the kingdom of darkness, which had long held me captive, was finally being threatened in me and its forces were fighting back.

When my tongue slid backwards and Gary said, "In the name of Jesus, come out of her," he was casting out a demon, an evil spirit that had been influencing my thoughts and words and actions for perhaps my entire life! No wonder that part of the experience was so intense. The evil spirit did not want to leave, and its eviction caused my body to tremble violently. Prior to that day, I had not believed in demons, but I could not deny that a sinister and controlling force of darkness had been dramatically removed from my life when Gary told it to leave in Jesus' name. The wonderful in-filling I experienced that day was the baptism of the Holy Spirit.

Throughout the whole experience, Gary and I were completely protected. Even though we broke several security rules and guards patrolled the area around us, eavesdropping on conversations and scrutinizing every action, no one came near us. Gary should never have been allowed inside the prison to see me, and he was not supposed to have touched me in any way. Even by putting one finger on my forehead, he had broken a rule. According to policy, the guards should have called for a medic when they saw me lying on the ground. But it was as if we were invisible to everyone, hidden by an unseen hand.

Then, the sharp voice of a guard interrupted my life-changing spiritual encounter. "Visiting hours are over! Everybody inside!" Gary helped me up from the ground, and we walked back into the visiting room so that he could go through the check-out process. He went back out into the free world, where his friend, Mark, had been waiting in the car, praying for Gary's visit with me. And I, on the other hand, went back into prison population, stunned and amazed. I stayed fairly quiet that evening, pondering what had happened to me—full of questions, but unable to doubt.

I was astounded and curious and grateful all at the same time. I knew I was drastically different inside. A powerful and fundamental exchange had taken place in the core of my being when "something evil left me and something wonderful filled me." But my dramatic encounter had left me with more questions than answers. Was it another experience like the one in California, one I might never understand, or had I really received the baptism of the Holy Spirit? Had God really begun to bring lasting change to my life? Or was I going to be labeled just another inmate with "jailhouse religion"? I could not answer those questions that night, but I somehow drifted off to sleep despite their running back and forth through my mind.

The next day, I recorded my recollection of Gary's incredible visit:

2/22/93: Sunday an angel came bearing a God-sent gift. I was in church. At 1:50, they came and got me for a visit. I didn't have my I.D. card, so I sprint-walked to the dorm. My heart was racing, but I was not nervous. It was 2:00 when I got there. Gary was talking to a guard. My palms were sweaty and my pulse was out of control. I think this was all spiritual.

We found a corner bench in the yard. Almost as soon as Gary sat down, he asked if I'd been baptized in the Holy Spirit. I told him no. He asked if I wanted to receive right then. I said yes. We stood up; he prayed; I fell. He asked for God's anointing to come upon me.

After that, I knew "something" was leaving. My first reaction was that my tongue started drawing straight back in my throat. It was also numbing. It was starting to choke me, then the trembles started in my stomach, then radiated down my legs, up my chest and down my arms. It felt very violent (the word hideous *comes to mind). Gary kept praying, commanding it to leave in the name of Jesus. I felt my body almost convulse for what felt like forever. It was so deep, trying to hold on—hidden, yet clinging. My tremors very slowly subsided. I remember a strong wind passing through the trees before it left. I felt groaning inside of me— hideous. Then it took a minute or two for my tongue to loosen.*

It's hard to explain. I was stiff, very starched. I whispered, "Jesus."

Chapter 11

Word and Spirit

The next morning ushered in a brand-new day and a brand-new me. I awakened earlier than usual, surprised by a craving for something I had never tasted before. I was starving for the Word of God! Who could imagine it? *Me*, reading the Bible? I had always considered Bible reading the province of preachers and saintly senior citizens, but that morning my heart was ravenous for it. It was as if God had deposited in me while I slept a knowing, an unshakable conviction, that the answers and direction I desperately needed were in that Book.

I jumped out of my bunk and surveyed my locker for the black leather Bible that Mike had sent me. I found it quickly and hurried back to my bed, eager to read it until time to get ready for work. Even after years of church-going, I was only familiar with a few Bible stories. I remembered something about Daniel and a pit full of lions, something about Noah and a boat full of animals. But I knew nothing of individual verses or biblical principles or the life-changing truth in the big Book I held in my hands. I only knew that there was something in the Bible I *had* to have.

I could not get my Bible open fast enough, and when I did, I could not believe my eyes. The words were alive! I was astounded by their immediate impact on me. How could black letters on white pages be so full of life? I did not understand, yet I could sense power as I read them. The rhythm of the Scriptures was a heartbeat all its own, a pulse of hope and strength for me in a place where both were almost nonexistent.

Before long, I came to realize that I *must* have received the baptism of the Holy Spirit when Gary prayed for me. Yes, I knew I had received that baptism. Who else but the Holy Spirit could have placed this unexplainable hunger for the Bible inside of me? How else would I have been so quickly and easily convinced of its truth and power? How else would my inner chaos have turned to peace or my despair to hope? It all *had* to be of the work of the Holy Spirit.

He also started waking me around 5:00 A.M. almost every morning. The first day, He gave me the inspired idea that I could borrow a few moments of privacy in a bathroom shower stall. So I took my Bible, a prison-issued number 2 lead pencil and a few sheets of notebook paper into a stall, and threw my multi-colored robe across its door as a sign that the shower was in use. Unlike most people in the shower, I was not using soap and water and shampoo; I was simply looking for a place to be alone, apart from the pandemonium of prison, to start my day with the Holy Spirit, who was fast becoming my best friend.

Once behind the closed door, I strategically arranged a folded towel on the floor so that I would not have to sit directly on the cold, hard tile. I positioned my flip-flops to cushion my bare feet and protect them from fungus as I sat Indian-style. My Bible rested on my left knee, and my notebook paper sat on my right knee. With my pencil in hand, I was ready to take notes on everything I read.

As I did, the Holy Spirit taught me through the Word. He spoke, and I wrote what He said. I knew so little about the Bible, but I soon learned that every time a scripture seemed to "jump off the page," it was as if the Holy Spirit had an invisible highlighter and was marking certain verses He wanted me to read. I devoured them, even though I did not fully understand them. Every morning in the shower stall was like the first day of school. I was so excited about what I would learn during my "class" in the "School of the Spirit" that day. And every morning, without fail, the Holy Spirit met me in my shower stall sanctuary and taught me.

One of the first verses He pricked my heart with was John 8:32, which told me that the truth sets people free. I knew it was impossible to physically escape my environment, but the Bible said that I did not have to leave prison in order to experience true freedom—freedom on the inside. I took a quantum leap toward freedom when I experienced supernatural deliverance from evil spirits the day Gary prayed for me, and wrote about it several weeks after his visit:

3/6/93: Oh the changes in my life! Deliverance! Who would actually believe that I—me—would have demonic spirits inside, living, controlling. Okay, I said it. It did happen. So many people I know and love would never understand.

Deliverance was a jump-start on my journey to freedom, but it was the Word of God that steadily fueled me. I could maintain the freedom I had gained only as I lived according to the truth of His Word, so I continued to read and study and meditate as often and as intensely as I possibly could, realizing that something I never thought possible was actually happening—my heart was being changed.

All my life, I had been one to fully embrace anything new or exciting, and the Bible was no different. I had never done anything half-heartedly; I was an all-or-nothing girl. For years, I had tried to help myself or improve my life and nothing worked! I discovered that I could not escape my problems by traveling the globe; that expensive clothes could not change a bad self-image; that feelings of rejection could not be reversed by a boyfriend's affection; that all the wine in the world could not drown the pain inside of me; and that I could not come up with a prescription for peace, put joy on a credit card or write a check for the love I longed for.

Thinking back over the futility of every effort I had made to heal my own heart and break free from the invisible chains that held me captive long before I ever went to prison, I concluded that I only had one more choice. Just one, and it was my very last hope. I was out of options.

Standing in my cell, I took my Bible in my hands, looked at it and said, "Lord, this Book is either totally true, or it isn't true at all. Everything in it is either true or it's not. If You will teach me how to live out of this Book, I'll do it—even in a place like this."

Soon after praying that prayer, the Holy Spirit presented me with a remarkable opportunity to demonstrate that I meant what I said—that I really would live according to His Word if He would show me how. Early one morning, I stumbled across Matthew 5:44, and read: "But I say to you, love your enemies, bless those who curse you, and pray for those who spitefully use you and persecute you."

Oh no! I thought. *Do I really have to do this?* Immediately, my thoughts raced back to the courtroom and the day my guilty verdict was returned. I had replayed that scene in my mind more times than I could count. I had pondered it privately and shared it with others, each time with intensified vengeance. It did not take much to stoke the fire of anger in me toward the judge, the jury and the prosecuting attorneys. My bitter hatred had not waned or weakened since that day, but had only taken deeper root in my heart. I knew exactly where the Holy Spirit wanted me to start this process of applying the Word personally in the area of forgiving and blessing—with my enemies: Judge Faulk, the prosecutors and the twelve jurors whose decision had sent me to prison.

Because I was reading the Bible in bed that morning I once again rolled out of my bunk, knelt on my flip-flops and began to pray. At first, my prayer was hollow and mechanical: "Lord, I forgive the judge and the jury and the people who prosecuted me. I forgive them for the pain their decisions have caused me—and my family. I ask You to bless them and I pray for them." Because the Holy Spirit showed me that harboring unforgiveness is like drinking poison and hoping it will hurt someone else, I was relieved to have dealt with that situation and eager to move on to the next lesson.

To my surprise, the Holy Spirit wanted me to stay in "forgiveness and blessing" class. The next day in prayer, He led me again to forgive and bless all those same people. Eventually, we did move on to other lessons, but He did not release me from praying for my enemies and even added to the list the probation officer assigned to my case before I even went to prison. I prayed for them until the attitude of my heart matched the words of my mouth, until I genuinely felt forgiveness and compassion for them and until I truly wanted the Lord to bless their lives. As I released them in prayer, He released more freedom and peace to me.

By May 1993, I had grown to love both the Lord and His

Word with a passion that astounded me. He had done a fast work! Who could have imagined that the condescending, self-confident woman who arrived at Benton just four months earlier would ever write the following words in her journal:

> *5/93: There is no other life I want to lead but the one in Christ Jesus, putting my entire self under the submission of the Word of God.*

I was determined to do anything—anything—that would help me live my life in Christ Jesus. Certainly, the power of the Word was doing a great work in me and the process through which the Holy Spirit taught me to apply the Scriptures in practical ways through difficult circumstances fascinated me. He had also begun teaching me how to pray, and I prayed often and fervently. But I still needed more—more power, more communion with Him. I needed to go deeper.

I remembered the booklet I had seen on top of the trashcan before I met Gary, and reading in it, "When you don't know how to pray, pray in the Holy Spirit." What did that really mean? Did it mean praying in a foreign language the way Gary did? I didn't know, but I recalled something that happened to me the day he came to visit.

I believed I had been baptized with the Holy Spirit and remembered hearing two syllables inside of me as I stood to my feet after being on the ground: *eye-yah*. Could that one unusual word really be part of a spiritual prayer language? Would I really be praying in the Holy Spirit if I said it? Could my saying it bring me power and inner strength? I had no idea.

But I did know that Gary had exhibited a spiritual authority I had never seen before. I had definitely witnessed the dark side of spiritual power in my New Age experiences, but they only led to confusion, deception and bondage. For so many years I had been power-hungry by the world's definition. Now I was hungry for God's power, the power that was setting me free and would help set others free as well. I did not care how ridiculous I felt. I was determined to grow; and this "praying in the Spirit" could be exactly what I needed. If I sounded crazy doing it, then I would just sound crazy. What were they going to do, lock me up?

So I prayed that little word repeatedly, with my mind accusing me: "You sound really stupid." But I just kept doing it, believing I was praying in the Spirit even though I did not know what I was praying. I wrestled against thoughts that I was losing my mind and sometimes wondered if I really were. The struggle was intense, perhaps because the power of praying in the Spirit is so great.

One Sunday after a chapel service, a young inmate asked me to pray for her because she was having problems with her family. I gathered a few other inmates around her to help me pray. After I had prayed only a few sentences, I suddenly felt a "spiritual hiccup," and a stream of words I did not understand came flowing out of my mouth as though I had been speaking them all of my life. An entire vocabulary was released, and my two-syllable word seemed to be a perfectly natural part of it. Even though I did not know what the words meant and they did not sound like what Gary had spoken, I knew his words and mine were all somehow related. We were both speaking the language of the Spirit in ways our minds could never grasp, but our hearts understood completely.

I marveled at this explosion of God in me—God by His Word and God by His Spirit—doing the greatest miracle of all: *changing me.*

Chapter 12

From the Inside Out

In the midst of my internal revolution, I began to see evidence of God all around me. He was not only busy changing my heart; He was actively involved in the daily grind of my life within the walls of a federal prison—teaching me here, challenging me there, molding me, rearranging me and revealing His love in a multitude of unexpected ways.

He started by re-visiting an area in which He had dealt with me before, by taking me through the next stage of an elementary lesson: trust—the annihilation of self-sufficiency. My life-long independence had built such a stronghold of self-reliance that, in order to permanently dismantle it, the Lord worked in me by peeling one layer after another off of me—like wallpaper off the walls of an old house. Just when I thought I had surrendered all, He scraped again and revealed another place I was still depending on myself.

Before I went to prison, I reveled in my self-sufficiency and had everything I ever wanted or needed. My life was filled with material abundance, and what I did not have I bought. Sales associates at a well-known Dallas department store knew me by name, and I sometimes visited that store and bought things I didn't need *just to buy them*. Part of my arrogance was rooted in my ability to take care of myself, and one of the primary ways I related to other people was by buying them gifts because that always gave me the upper hand—I thought. Never comfortable receiving, I always wanted to be the giver—the one who *had,* not the one who *needed.* I had plenty of problems, but taking care of myself was not one of them.

Prisoners live limited lives, and one of the great frustrations of incarceration was that many things I wanted or thought I needed were not available. Every inmate was issued a tube of bad-tasting toothpaste, a cheap plastic toothbrush, ten envelopes, several sheets of paper and one pencil per month, but we had to buy everything else.

Benton had a commissary, which was the only place we could buy non-issued items. We were only permitted to go to the commissary one night per week, only on an assigned night and only during a specified two-hour time slot. If, for any reason, an inmate missed her opportunity to go to the commissary at her appointed time, she could not go again for another week. There were no make-up sessions, no rain checks, just the graceless "use it or lose it" policy that governed so many aspects of our lives.

During our weekly visits to the commissary, we bought everything from stamps to shampoo to junk food to laundry tokens to the flip-flops we wore in the shower. The commissary only carried one brand of many items, so our choices were terribly limited. On top of that, so many things common to the average American household, such as aerosol sprays and alcohol-based products (skin toner, mouthwash and other personal hygiene items) were forbidden in prison. Nothing was available in the top-of-the-line brands I normally used, but I soon discovered that even if I had been given the option to choose brand-name merchandise, I would not have had the money to purchase everything I wanted.

Each inmate had an account to which prison officials credited the money we earned on our jobs. Payday was once a month, at the end of the month, and all of our wages were deposited into our commissary accounts. In addition, our families or friends could send money for our accounts, but there was a limit to how much an individual could have.

I was shocked by how little I could purchase on a month's pay. Laundry tokens cost a quarter apiece, so at my hourly wage of seventeen cents, I had to work three hours just to earn enough money to wash and dry one load of clothes—and laundry tokens were only one small expense. Occasionally, the commissary sold bananas, and I craved fresh fruit, which was a treat to my taste buds compared to the food in the chow hall. I wanted to take advantage of the opportunity to eat something fresh and healthy, but bananas were also twenty-five cents each, an hour-and-a-half's worth of manual labor at the warehouse.

One of the worst things about the commissary was that we were never certain how much money was in our accounts because sometimes our paychecks were not posted exactly when we thought they would be. But, when it came to the availability of our funds, only the haphazard was consistent, so we never really knew.

One thing I did know though, was that the purchasing procedure at the commissary was terribly tedious. With my retail experience and knack for efficiency, I had little patience for the multi-step process I had to endure each week. It all seemed so unnecessary as I waited in line to get an order form with a number on it and then marked it with the items I needed. I then waited for someone to call the number on the form so that I could slide it through a tiny slot to a worker who would gather everything I requested, and then gave my form and my purchases to an officer who brought up my account on a computer screen and rang up my total.

Sometimes, an inmate progressed all the way to the checkout area only to be informed that she did not have enough money to cover what she needed to buy. Being accustomed to always having more than enough money, I was astounded one night when that happened to me.

I showed up for my weekly shopping trip with my prison-issued, see-through mesh bag for commissary purchases. I really needed several items that week and went through every laborious step of the process. When the officer looked at my account on the computer screen that night, he said, "Forsythe, you're out of luck. You don't have any money. You can't get a thing." I was mortified. I could never remember having a zero balance in an account that bore my name!

Being told that I did not have resources to even provide myself with the basic necessities was like having nothing— and then having, well, doubly nothing. Not only did I not have the things I needed, I had no way to get them. I walked back to my cell that night with my empty bag feeling as though I lived in the bottom of a pit, and its floor had suddenly dropped ten feet deeper.

As I entered my cell, I saw a miracle-in-a-pile on my bunk. While I was at the commissary, someone had slipped into my cell and left me exactly what I needed—the very things I tried to buy. The giver left an anonymous note that read: "Love your neighbor as yourself. Matthew 22:39." Tears streamed down my face as I realized how deeply the Lord knew my tiniest practical needs and met them at the perfect moment. As hard as I tried not to cry in prison, that night I allowed liquid gratitude to flow freely down my cheeks.

I had rotated one-hundred-and-eighty-degrees from being able to take care of myself. I couldn't! And my family and friends could not help me either. The Lord dealt a lethal blow to my self-sufficiency so I could see that I was not, and had never been, sufficient at all. I could never have imagined not having the money to buy a few inexpensive items at a prison commissary, but the Lord stepped into my life that night to say, "Mary, I can do what you cannot. I know precisely what you need and *you can trust Me.*"

Up to that point in my prison experience, my arrogance had so often been confronted by challenging experiences that broke my pride because they were so hard or so humiliating—working for Mr. Isaacs, enduring strip searches and having to submit to random urinalyses, to name a few. This time, my pride was not broken by difficulty, but melted by a tender demonstration of the Lord's lavish love and intimate attention toward me.

Being given the supplies I needed from the commissary was a dramatic display of the Lord's provision that showed me clearly how helpless I really was and how deeply I must depend on Him for everything. As I learned to trust Him, I began to see that I could trust Him not only for my needs, but also for His provision all around me in a variety of less-obvious ways.

One of the most nerve-racking aspects of prison life was that everything about my physical existence was monotonous to an extreme. My personal routine was the same every day: the food never varied too much from week to week; and my stifling surroundings never changed. I even looked at the same drab colors on everything from uniforms to bunk beds to the point that I thought my eyes might atrophy.

The Lord knew how hungry I was for variety—and how small the chances were that I would find much in prison. For example, the tap water was the worst I had ever tasted, so one of my priority purchases at the commissary was a one-gallon jug of bottled water. I tried to buy water every week, and every week I lugged it back to my cell. I bought the same items at the same time on the same night of every week and carried them from the commissary to my cell along the same sidewalk and put them in the same place in my locker once I got there. One night, He gave me the idea to me to carry my jug of water in my left hand instead of my right hand. That tiny adjustment, which most people might never have stopped to consider, provided a spark of variety I not only noticed, but even found myself excited about. The monotony was *that* severe.

Even in the midst of the dull reality of prison, there were still occasions we wanted to celebrate—a birthday, a baptism or a send-off for an inmate the night before her release. I knew I could no longer throw the kinds of parties I had given in my former life, but I quickly learned from other inmates how to transform simple foods from the commissary into special-occasion meals. For instance, we put a can of chili and some processed cheese spread into a bag of crushed corn chips, put a towel on top of that mixture and heated it with an iron. Before I went to prison, I would never have eaten such a recipe. But there, it was a delicacy.

The Holy Spirit knew we needed fellowship and celebration. As I thought about our chili-cheese concoction, I realized that I could trust Him to cause creativity to transform the ordinary into the special so that we would have bright moments in the midst of a dark environment, light moments in the midst of heavy, oppressive surroundings.

No sooner than the Spirit began teaching me to trust Him to provide for material and social needs, He went beyond helping me put names and faces together at small celebrations and chose a true friend for me, an inmate I had met not long after I arrived at Benton—a sweet-spirited Christian woman, a few years older than I. I wondered when I met her, how it was that she had lived in such a difficult place for several months already and yet there was not a hint of hardness in her. Her name was Liz, and she soon became one of my closest friends and prayer partners—someone who shared her needs and concerns with me, and I with her, so that we could pray with and for each other. I felt that the Lord had ordained our friendship—that He had specifically chosen us to be friends and called us to walk a portion of the prison journey together.

Not only was Liz someone I could share the Word with, pray with and face the day-to-day battles of prison life with, she was another expression of the Lord's provision for me. There were at least two domestic chores I had never mastered: ironing and bed-making. Where some inmates were accomplished enough to iron stars, letters or geometric patterns into their uniform shirts, I could not manage to simply get the wrinkles out of mine and usually looked somewhat rumpled. Liz, however, ironed like a professional. In motherly fashion, she began ironing my uniforms for me so that I would look and feel neat. Once she did, I realized what she already knew—that it was extremely important to make the effort to present myself as best as I possibly could, even in prison.

Liz was also an expert at the art of making beds—tight sides, tucked corners. Guards inspected our cells each day while we were at work, and an entire cell could be reprimanded if one inmate's bunk was not made properly. As hard as I tried, my bed always looked like someone was still in it! I left for work every morning knowing that my bed was not quite up to standards, but also knowing I had done my best. Many afternoons, I returned to see my bed made perfectly. Time after time, without ever saying a word, Liz came by my cell after I left for the warehouse, and fixed it for me.

Another way the Lord intervened in my everyday circumstances was to provide me with a strategically located cell. Soon after I went to Benton, I had moved from the first floor cell, where I watched the pink rosebush outside my window, to a second floor cell, where I stayed for all but ten days of the remainder of my prison term.

When I first moved into my new cell, I was shocked to realize that it had no view outside its tiny window. The windows in all the other cells offered at least a snapshot of sky or a bush, but not this one. When I looked out its window, I saw not even the tip of a tree branch. I saw nothing but the faded red tile roof of the adjacent dormitory. Just a glimpse of something—*anything*—that was not government property would have helped. But day after day, no matter how hard I craned my neck or how tall I stood on my tip-toes, nothing. Nothing but a jailhouse roof.

But I quickly noticed the redemptive aspect of that cell's location when the Holy Spirit showed me that if I slept with my head toward the door, the bathroom light shone in just enough for me to read my Bible during the night. (The other inmates slept with their heads as far away from the door as possible because guards walked the halls at night with heavy footsteps, jangling keys and making other loud noises. Being even a few feet from the door helped decrease the disturbance of the nighttime activity.) When I held my Bible at the right angle, the restrictions of "lights out" at a certain time did not restrict my time in the Word because the light was just bright enough for me to make out the words on the pages. What that cell lacked in terms of a view, it made up for in functionality.

The other amazing thing about my cell was that it was next to a mop closet. None of the cells had doors, which was infinitely nerve-racking because it meant that an inmate never had—*could* never have—a moment's privacy. Even people walking casually down the hall could see everything she did.

Even though the mop closet was filthy and smelly, it had a door—a precious barrier no one could see through—and I made the most of it. The Holy Spirit knew I needed a room with a door, a private place. He knew that Benton was filled with women who needed someone with whom they could share the secrets of their hearts, women who needed prayer. Perhaps they had been tortured by sexual abuse during their childhood, or carried the silent shame of an abortion, or struggled with thoughts of suicide or suffered from the torment of holding unforgiveness in their hearts.

By then, the Holy Spirit had healed me enough that I wanted to help others. There was no end to the private pain they bore and once they found out someone was willing to help many of them sought it. The mop closet provided a safe environment in which we could share and pray and where the Holy Spirit could deal with an inmate without her being observed by curious eyes and becoming the subject of the next day's gossip.

My proximity to the mop closet was like having an office next to my house! Not only did I use it to minister to and pray for other inmates, it also became a meeting place for several Christians almost nightly, after 9:00 P.M. count (a four-times daily process in which guards counted inmates, cell by cell, to make sure no one had escaped and everyone was accounted for). Because we did not have to be in our cells until at least 10:30 P.M., we spent that time praying and praising and worshiping. Night after night, the Holy Spirit's presence was sweet and powerful in the mop closet, always providing glorious endings to grueling days.

Chapter 13

Beginning to Bloom

I began my time at Benton with a fierce determination to keep as much distance as possible between myself and others. It was hard to find nice people in prison! In the beginning, I did not try, or even want, to get to know anyone because I was not planning to be there long and because I considered myself so far "above" the other inmates. But once the pardon did not materialize, I realized that all the women at Benton were going to be my neighbors—seven days a week, twenty-four hours a day—for much longer than I had expected. Whether I liked it or not, these inmates were the population of my life. I finally resigned myself to the fact that I had to live with everyone, but I did not have to be friends with anyone.

Besides, Mike was still my best friend. We spoke often by phone and he visited regularly on weekends, but as my heart absorbed the reality that our entire relationship would consist of nothing more than phone calls and not-so-private times together in the midst of a prison yard, I had to admit that the arrangement was hardly fulfilling. Our short weekend visits were a drastic departure from the months we lived together and often spent twenty-four hours a day with each other. I was always glad to see him, but the longer I stayed in prison and he stayed in the free world, our lives became more different and our visits more difficult.

My trip to prison had proven to be so much more than the two-week adventure I expected. I found it to be, instead, an arduous journey that would not end for many months—and I had to ask myself the question that tore my heart in two: Would Mike really wait for me? I did not know, but the Holy Spirit was changing my heart, and I knew that I had to exercise my trust by releasing my future with Mike to Him. I did not know what would become of us. I only knew that I had to put my desire for us to stay together into the hands of the Lord and let the Holy Spirit take the situation from there.

In the process, the Holy Spirit changed everything, including my commitment to make it through prison on my own, and melted my steely resolve to isolate myself (as much as isolation was possible in prison!). The more I understood and received His love for me, the more my perception of other people changed. I began to "cut them some slack" and even to feel compassion toward them.

About the same time, I heard a sermon on television. It was based on the familiar old saying, "Bloom where you're planted," and as I heard the minister speak those words to an audience of thousands, I knew that the Holy Spirit had aimed them straight at the heart of one woman listening alone in a Texas prison: me. But my first thought was, *Lord, Not here! No way! Look where I am! How am I supposed to "bloom" in the middle of this prison?*

As usual, the Holy Spirit answered my question and I soon realized that the more I learned through my adventures with Him, the more I wanted to tell other people what He was teaching me. Hey! That was a way to bloom where I was planted!

I started by developing an "underground press." But in order for that venture to succeed, I needed help. Every month, I used all of the paper issued to me to write multiple copies of a lesson or truth I had learned, and it took all of my envelopes to mail those "newsletters" to family and friends. But I never had enough paper or envelopes or stamps to send as many newsletters as I wanted to, so other inmates donated some of theirs. None of them had any more than I did, but as they each gave what they could, I always had the supplies I needed. Soon, my mailing list grew, and because of the generosity of others, I always had enough newsletters to mail to everyone on the expanding list.

The underground press allowed me to contribute to people's lives in valuable but intangible ways, feeding them spiritual food since I had nothing material to give. Helping other people infused me with life and strength as it allowed me to reach beyond prison walls to share what the Spirit was doing within them.

With the underground press in full operation to communicate with people "on the outside," I realized that I did not have a means through which to share with the inmates inside prison walls—and I was going to be planted there for a good while. Where I had once made great effort to avoid other inmates, I now sought them out on purpose and began to gather a handful of women who were hungry for the truth and started teaching a Bible study for them. Whatever the Spirit taught me, I turned around and taught them. As He revealed a truth to my heart, I meditated on it, prayed about it, looked up scriptures about it and then shared it with others. Whatever I learned, those women learned too. I really *had* changed!

But all of us had a lot to learn in the area of tithing. When I first discovered the truth about tithing, my immediate thought was, *Give ten percent? I only make seventeen cents an hour and I never even see it!* We inmates must have been among the lowest paid workers in the entire United States, and there were times some women could barely afford even the inexpensive basic necessities sold at the commissary. But I soon discovered that tithing was a joy. It was another way for me to reach beyond the confines I was in and participate in what God was doing through others. Regardless of how much or how little money I had, I determined that I would be obedient to the Lord and give a percentage of my meager income to a local church or to one of the ministers who held meetings at Benton.

In order to do anything with our money besides make purchases at the commissary, we had to go to the mailroom and fill out a request form instructing the prison officials where to send a specified amount of money and for what purpose. Yes, tithing was a logistical hassle and the amount seemed insignificant, but the Lord was more interested in the attitude of my heart than in the size of my gift.

Learning about tithing and other biblical principles began to affect the way we lived. The Bible study was more than just a group of women passing their time in jail. It was part of the process we needed in order to build new lives for ourselves according to the blueprint of God's Word.

Because there were few secrets in prison, other inmates

soon heard about our Bible study. Some were curious, some were cautious, some were skeptical and some were thrilled. One by one, the Holy Spirit began to show me which women shared "like precious faith" (2 Peter 1:1), which ones were desperate for Him and which ones I might be able to count as friends. He gave me a desire to do even more than teach a Bible study. I felt that He wanted to gather a "Remnant Group," and that several of us were to get together every Saturday night for the simple purpose of being with Him. It was in that little group that I, and others, not only bloomed but flourished.

When I mentioned the idea to a few other women, they were delighted. As much as we appreciated the various ministers who came to Benton, we always needed more of the power of corporate prayer and worship, even if there were only a few of us. So we made plans to meet together, just us prisoners. Each week we prayed and asked the Holy Spirit to show us where we could meet without interruption, and He did.

From the very beginning, the Remnant Group was special. About five of us formed the core of the group, but at times as many as six or seven others joined us. Although I met and ministered to many women, those in the Remnant Group were among my closest friends. In spite of my determination to not make friends in prison, I ended up with closer friendships than I could have ever imagined. As I looked at the women the Holy Spirit brought together, I could not help but marvel at the way He seemed to gather a small slice of the body of Christ right there at Benton. We were a beautiful mix of women of different cultures, backgrounds, ages and experiences—so much more than a bunch of "religious" people in prison in Texas. We were the righteousness of God in Christ; we were His passionate worshipers; we were a mighty, if small, army of praying warriors. And we were as vibrant and as free in Him as any group of believers anywhere.

Week after week, we looked forward to our meetings with eager anticipation. Each time the Holy Spirit showed us exactly where to meet and what we should do when everyone arrived. He always directed us to the right place, and every meeting was different. We saw so many facets of His character, His power and His compassion as He led us in fresh, new ways every Saturday night. We loved the incredible variety and spontaneity of the Holy Spirit and delighted in our diversity as we followed Him together. Uncertainty was always certain in our meetings and was even comfortable because we knew the Spirit was leading us. We could never predict what our times together would include, but we always showed up with hearts that hungered for His presence.

When we gathered, we simply waited on the Holy Spirit until He revealed His plans for the meeting. We made ourselves available to respond to anything He asked of us. Sometimes He directed us by reminding someone of a scripture or by giving one of us an impression or by showing someone a vision. Always, the Holy Spirit's presence was sweet and secure. After a meeting on June 2, 1994, I remembered our meeting and wrote about it in my journal:

06/03/94: Last night was a powerful prayer group. We gathered in the education room. We began praising, worshipping and ministering to the Lord. It was as if the Holy Spirit was in the room waiting for us. I could feel His presence as we walked in the room. We prayed in the Spirit and sang to Him. I prayed for each woman at her feet. Theresa was consumed with His presence as she knelt, praising Him.

The heart of the Remnant Group seemed to be praying for different nations. Often the Holy Spirit assigned specific countries or people groups to us, and we followed Him in prayer for those places and those people. Sometimes an inmate would see, in her mind's eye, the shape or outline of a country, as if she were looking at a map. From behind prison bars, we reached all the way around the world as we touched the nations in intercession.

Almost always, we also prayed for the people in positions of leadership and authority at Benton—the warden, the other officials, the chaplain and the guards. We did this out of obedience to 1 Timothy 2:1, 2 which says, "Therefore I exhort first of all that supplications, prayers, intercessions, and giving of thanks be made for all men, for kings and all who are in authority, that we may lead a quiet and peaceable life in all godliness and reverence." We also prayed for our fellow inmates at Benton and in other prisons, knowing how miserable they were and understanding the harsh realities of their lives better than anyone else could.

The Holy Spirit was always faithful to us, always hearing our prayers, always helping us and strengthening us. He constantly surprised us as He orchestrated our times together, leading us to do everything from sitting silently before Him, to shouting for joy, to weeping over unsaved people in remote regions, to helping one of our own women deal with the painful places in her heart. There were nights when the Holy Spirit called us to war in prayer over a particular situation and times He allowed us to simply worship and be captivated by His beauty. Whatever He wanted to do, we gladly and eagerly embraced.

Our common desperation for Him united us. We grew to trust each other as we sought Him together and found our

Remnant Group sisters to be not only true friends, but intercessors, confidants, cheerleaders and burden-sharers.

I could not believe how much my heart had changed. The Holy Spirit had taken me—an arrogant, fiercely independent woman determined to keep my distance from anyone else—and handpicked a few choice friends for me. They were His jewels behind bars, and He ordained us to walk together with Him through the most difficult days of our lives.

Chapter 14

Deeper

No matter how many good friends I had, there were aspects of my life I needed to deal with alone—heart issues and attitudes that could not be wrestled with in a Bible study or a Remnant Group meeting. They had to be confronted by the Holy Spirit in the privacy of my own soul.

After I had been in prison several months and the Holy Spirit had been working on many foundational areas of my life, it was time to go deeper—time to dismantle an internal fortress that, for most of my life, had kept Him at arm's length and caused me to resist His presence and the work He longed to do in me. It was time to expose and break my rebellion.

I suppose I had been rebellious all of my life. I was the kind of child about whom people remarked, "She sure has an independent streak," and who never asked for help because I wanted to do it myself—whatever "it" was. My rebellion and independence were like fruit hanging on a tree, separate but related products of the same root—pride. And that root had to be pulled out of the soil of my life so that its fruit would stop showing up in my attitudes and behavior.

I was desperate for the Lord and had read in 1 Peter 5:5 that, "God resists the proud, but gives grace to the humble." By the time I read that truth, I was fully aware that pride had been a problem for me all of my life and I thought, *Oh no! I've got to do something about this pride. I don't need God to resist me—I need grace.* I had to learn how to humble myself.

Because the Spirit wanted to teach me the beauty of humility and joy of obedience, He had already placed me in the perfect classroom—the warehouse. I was still working there with Mr. Isaacs as my boss and still bristling inside every time he demanded that I do a job his way when I wanted to do it mine. After all, I was accustomed to making my own rules for more than thirty years, and I did not want to submit to higher laws. But the Holy Spirit began to teach me that obedience does not begin and end with external actions. It starts with a humble heart attitude and ends with behavior that honors the position *of* authority, not necessarily the person *in* authority.

About that same time, an important book found its way into my hands—a book that would be key to unlocking my understanding of submission and authority. The principles in *Spiritual Authority* (now entitled *Authority and Submission*), by Watchman Nee, invaded my life and turned my thinking upside down. As I read it, I began to see that the Lord was so much more interested in my heart than in my performance. He was looking for true humility more than He was looking to see how I moved a mop.

It took months of working in the warehouse for me to face the truth that my pride and haughty attitude were sin. Pride had blinded me to my own faults and kept me from seeing how hard my heart was. I did not know how arrogant, how bitter, how independent or how rebellious I was. I had not realized that my attitude toward Mr. Isaacs did not honor the Lord, and in fact, that He had placed that man in a position of authority in my life, and it did not matter whether I wanted to submit to him or not. It did not matter whether he was a good boss or a bad boss; he was *the* boss.

I remembered one of my first impressions when I met Mr. Isaacs, a quick assessment that I was more highly educated than he, and that in my pre-prison life I probably made more money in one month than he did in a whole year. How judgmental! What a work the Spirit was doing in my heart during my time at the warehouse as He revealed to me the power of humility, which meant obeying with both my heart and actions those who were in positions of authority over me. Day after day, the Holy Spirit orchestrated circumstances that allowed me to choose whether I would simply obey *on* the outside or obey *from* the inside. It was a grueling time as He dealt with me in an area that was especially difficult for me.

By summer, I just could not take the warehouse environment anymore. Something had to change. I had spent hours in the stifling Texas heat painting warehouse equipment, and my skin was like old, dry leather from being in the sun. I had carried countless heavy bags of food on my back several days a week, and the manual labor was taking its toll on me—but more than anything I could not stand baiting any more rattraps!

I felt the Lord's hand on my heart like a potter's hand on a lump of clay. He was shaping me, and the more I resisted Him, the more pressure I felt from the process. He spoke to my heart one July day, helping me understand His work in me:

7/17/93: Do not fight the Spirit as you did when, as a child, you began to learn to swim and fought the water.

The water has the strength and ability to make you float if you remain still.

There was my answer; I would have to "remain still and cooperate with the Spirit." I would have to learn. I would have to relinquish more of the control I kept trying to exert in my life. Several months earlier, I had prayed, "Lord, if you will teach me how to live out of this Book [the Bible], I will," and I meant it. This was another chance to do that. It would require more obedience and more humility, but it would lead to more freedom and to a more intimate, vibrant relationship with Him.

However, obedience was only one of the areas in which the Holy Spirit was working in my life, and I was amazed by how much He could do all at once! As He was training me to submit and honor and obey, He also began to reveal that He had a plan for my life—a plan that was totally different from the plans I had made for myself. He started showing me that I was made *for* a purpose and *with* a purpose. He was calling me to do something special somehow, somewhere, someday— and He gave me the faith to believe it:

7/18/93: I prayed, "Lord, make me unyielding to my calling and give me an undivided heart."

I knew that I could not stand firm in my calling or have an undivided heart if I were not fully submitted to the Lord. Being in the warehouse was almost unbearable, but as much as I wanted out, I also wanted to learn everything He wanted to teach me in that classroom of the School of the Spirit. I wanted to leave, but not with a single assignment undone or a single lesson unlearned.

Mr. Isaacs had a reputation for not allowing his inmates

to change job assignments. He simply did not release people from the warehouse until they were released from prison. I began to pray. While I was waiting for the Lord to answer my prayer to reassign me (almost six months of praying!), He continued to give me opportunities to understand what obedience really meant in practical, everyday situations.

One day after I had worked in the warehouse for about a year, I was moving pallets with the forklift, and once again Mr. Isaacs instructed me to do the job in a seemingly nonsensical manner. He wanted me to move them one way, but I wanted to move them another way and was certain that my way was better. But by then, the Spirit had softened my heart and convinced me of the importance of humble submission. Sitting on the forklift, finally refusing my typical rebellious attitude, I surrendered to Him and said, "I'll do it. I'll do it his way. Lord, I will agree with him in my actions and honor him in my heart."

The following day, an amazing turn of events took place. Mr. Isaacs called me into his office, and my heart pounded within me as I wondered what his next demand would be. I had never seen an inmate called into his office before, and I reasoned, *This has to be something really big.* When Mr. Isaacs closed the door, I could hardly breathe and thought I might faint before I ever found out why he wanted to see me. I managed to compose myself, and heard him simply say: "Forsythe, if you want to be released from here, find another job and I'll sign the papers. Now get back to work."

Chapter 15

Excellent on the Inside

Thank You, Lord! I thought when I found out I had been assigned to a new job. After Mr. Isaacs' uncharacteristic offer to release me from the warehouse when I found another place to work, I quickly got busy looking for somewhere I thought would offer better working conditions. I prayed, believing that the Lord had arranged for me to be able to leave the warehouse, and knowing He would open the next door.

According to prison procedure, I had contacted the officer responsible for the job that seemed to be right for me—working as an orderly in one of the prison dorms. I knew that job changes became effective only when they were posted on the daily "call-out sheet," which was one form of official communication between inmates and prison authorities. We were required to check that sheet every morning, and on it, we received orders to change cells or bunks or report for a medical visit, which might have been requested so long ago that it was no longer necessary.

The only thing I was interested in on the call-out sheet was my job change and when it would take effect. When it did, I would report to my new job that same day. Sometimes the call-out sheet was not legible or would disappear because an inmate had taken it; but if we did not follow its instructions, we could be punished.

For me, the worst thing about the call-out sheet was that it was just one more reminder that I had zero control over my own life. That simple piece of paper encapsulated the seemingly arbitrary authority that ruled my everyday existence. I never knew what was going to happen when, and that frustrated me to no end. But when I saw my name, my I.D. number and a job change order, I was relieved and thankful.

What a year it had been in the warehouse! I had learned so much. The Holy Spirit had begun to align my will with His in order to free me from my past and prepare me for my future. I was grateful to be re-assigned and knew I would appreciate my new job because it would be much less demanding both time-wise and physically.

Being an orderly in one of the dormitories was, in my opinion, one of the prison's most desirable jobs. No one was allowed to be in the dorms during work hours unless she worked as an orderly or was unassigned for medical reasons. The duties of an orderly did not require the entire workday to complete, so I would be able to "legally" spend some time alone in my cell after I completed my tasks each day and still be paid for a full work week.

At first, I was an orderly in my own dorm, Jackson 1. Then, one day a drug rehabilitation counselor asked me if I wanted to work in Jackson 2, the dorm that housed inmates incarcerated on drug convictions. I took that job because its only responsibility was to clean the counselor's office, which would allow me even more free time. I swept, dusted, washed windows and emptied trash. When I finished my daily work, which was often before lunch, I was allowed to return to my cell and enjoy the gift of solitude for a few hours every afternoon.

Up until that time, I had primarily relied upon the Holy Spirit to teach me through the Scriptures and through books I checked out from the small chapel library. But now He began to use men and women from the outside world to teach me and to help me grow spiritually. Several ministers, including Ben, Betty and Herman, held meetings at the prison every week.

Consistency was rare in prison, and the inmates who attended services with them found a strange comfort in the simple knowledge that Ben would be there on Tuesday nights, Betty would be there on Thursday nights and Herman would be there on Sunday nights. I rarely missed one of their meetings, and neither did the Holy Spirit! These ministers knew how important it was to cooperate with the Spirit and to welcome His presence with attitudes of worship and thanksgiving. Each in their own style facilitated an atmosphere that allowed us to encounter the Holy Spirit in unique ways. I learned so much from each one, even though their approaches to ministry were quite different.

Ben was a tender-hearted, hard-working, generous man who came every Tuesday night to minister to just a handful of inmates. Each week, he brought his Bible, his guitar, an amplifier, a wooden music stand and tattered music sheets for us to use while singing. Without fail, we knew the presence of the Holy Spirit was with us in a special way when Ben led a meeting. He loved the Lord with all of his heart, and that love overflowed to us. He allowed the gifts of the Holy Spirit to operate freely in our midst and helped us learn how to function in those gifts. We stumbled at times, but Ben always encouraged us by saying, "You can't make a mistake here."

I also enjoyed Betty, a tiny fireball of a preacher, who arrived each week with a hug for each one of us. She brought the passion and zeal of the Lord in one hand and a large dose of unconditional love in the other. At the same time, she preached with a fervor and conviction that challenged us and inspired us and called us to holiness. She knew our living conditions were extremely difficult, but still encouraged us not to live beneath God's standards. As hard as it was, I knew she was right.

And there was Herman, a serious, steady, rock-of-Gibraltar type of minister who taught us about spiritual warfare, deliverance and prayer. Every week, he brought a two-edged sword of encouragement, using one side to cut the residue of my past off of me and the other to prod me toward a promising future. Week after week he said to me, "God's got something for you outside these walls." Oh, how I needed to hear that!

In addition, two friends from a local church, Marilyn and Norma, led Bible studies every week and always showed up with motherly affection and acceptance for us. They not only brought the Word inside the prison walls, they also supported us from the outside with their ladies' prayer group, who prayed for us weekly.

Also, we could always count on Weldon, who smiled constantly and never tired of preaching about living an overcoming life. He told me every time he visited that I was called and chosen and justified—words that made me feel special in a place that didn't exactly breed affirmation!

Another minister who visited regularly, but not weekly, was a soft-spoken, humble man named Don Dickerman. His ministry was devoted to prisoners, and Benton was only one of the many prisons where he ministered throughout the

United States. He always came with a smile and a joke, offering the unique encouragement that came from hearing stories about other inmates in other institutions. Signs and wonders usually followed the messages Don shared with us, but even more special was the fact that he always treated us with dignity and respect, never attaching to us the stigmas that always accompany prisoners.

Beyond those experiences, I had increased access to radio and television because of my job in the dorm, and the Holy Spirit used broadcast media to teach, equip and train me even more. Before work one morning, I sensed the Holy Spirit telling me to go into the television room and turn the set to a certain channel. When I did, I saw on the screen a dark-haired woman with a low voice, preaching in a straightforward and practical way. That woman was Joyce Meyer, and over the next months and years, the Lord used her ministry to help me gain strength and stability.

Joyce was the one who had taught about "blooming where you're planted," which had helped me greatly, but I also learned another important lesson from her—a lesson about having "an excellent spirit." Benton was a depressing place, and an air of laziness and apathy continually hung in its atmosphere. Most people simply wanted to pass their time there and carry out their responsibilities with as little effort as possible. Even though I had always worked hard and spent long hours at my businesses, prison's lethargic environment began to affect even me. I knew that in order for me to have an excellent spirit in those circumstances, I had to have the power that only came from the Word and the Spirit.

I discovered that I needed to be excellent from the inside out. I could not simply "get the job done"; I needed to have an attitude of excellence toward everything I did—prison or no prison! After hearing the message about an excellent spirit, I knew I was being called to live above my "just get by" environment. I wanted to live differently—and that meant *I* had to change. I soon had some opportunities to practice making heart attitude adjustments that would reflect an excellent spirit.

One day I was cleaning the windows of the television room as part of my job in the dorm, rushing through the task so I could return to my cell. The Holy Spirit spoke to me and said, "Mary, you missed a section." A quick survey of the windows revealed that, indeed, I had completely skipped one pane of glass. I responded in my heart, *It's just a window. It's just one pane. Besides, within five minutes a bunch of inmates will be putting their hands all over it and messing it up again.*

Then it hit me: I was in the middle of a test. I knew I had to go back and clean that section of glass, so I squirted the window cleaner and rubbed that pane with a paper towel and made sure it sparkled as much as the others did. I was pleased with the result not because the windows looked nice, but because I had taken my first intentional step toward walking in excellence.

I also learned that I could not have an excellent spirit and indulge the desires of my flesh at the same time. One of my flesh's favorite meals was a special dinner that was only served one Sunday night per month and was the only meal at which I could accurately identify the meat dish: fried chicken. It seemed to be every inmate's favorite meal, the one people did not skip. I never saw such greed and jockeying for position as I did when we were released from the dorm for chow time on those Sunday evenings.

Many times, Liz and I spent Sunday afternoons watching Christian television and gleaning everything we could from various ministers. I often enjoyed a dynamic minister from

Dallas, who preached and taught the Word with power and in ways that always spoke to my heart personally. The Sunday broadcasts of his sermons began a few minutes before dinner call was announced over the public address system, so I was faced with a tough choice on fried chicken nights!

One afternoon, Liz and I decided that we were handing our flesh a victory every time we chose to join the stampede of inmates rushing for fried chicken and left the opportunity to hear the preaching. We committed to deny ourselves the best meal of the month, believing that as we fed ourselves with spiritual food, we were investing in inner excellence.

The excellent spirit I so wanted to develop was challenged in a particularly difficult way one Saturday morning. I walked out of my dorm, headed to the track for some exercise. As I exited my building and started through the courtyard where dozens of inmates had congregated for their morning smoke, a guard yelled, "Forsythe! Come here!" I approached her and she thrust a small broom, a dustpan and an empty trash bag into my hands. Glancing toward a nearby drainage pit that doubled as a gigantic outdoor ashtray, she ordered, "Take these. Get down there. And clean up those cigarette butts."

My mind retorted, *"This is not my job."* But I had already taken a class in submission and obedience, and I knew I had to resist that thought, respect the guard's position of authority and obey her orders.

With every eye in the courtyard on me, I lifted the heavy steel grate over the pit and lowered myself about five feet to the bottom. It was damp and smelly and muddy and covered with still-smoldering cigarette butts. The broom I had been given was shorter and smaller than most brooms, so I had to bend over in order to scoop the butts into the dustpan and then dump them into the trash bag. With no way to avoid the stench of the pit, I swept as quickly as my arms would go so that I could get out and breathe fresh air again.

I will never make it through this disgusting job, I thought. Then the Holy Spirit spoke to me and said, "Praise Me." I replied under my breath, "You have *got* to be kidding!" But by that time, I knew how strategic He is and reminded myself that if He was asking me to do something, He was doing so in order to bring life and freedom. I did not burst into the *Hallelujah* chorus, but I did muster a hum. After a few minutes, I began to sing a quiet song, just loud enough for my own ears to hear it.

Singing did not alter the nastiness of the pit, but it did take my focus off of it and cause me to rise above my circumstances. I learned the power of praise in that pit as I declared my victory over a difficult situation, even though I was still standing in the middle of the battlefield.

I finally finished my assignment and began crawling out of the pit when the Holy Spirit said to me, "Mary, look over your right shoulder." When I did, I saw five cigarette butts in the far corner of the pit. I knew what to do; to be excellent I had to pick up those remaining butts, even though no one was looking and no one would ever know whether I got them or not.

When I had swept up the last five butts, I climbed out of the pit reeking of smoke and with my boots covered in mud, painfully aware of the smug stares of the inmates watching, undoubtedly wondering how "that Christian" had responded to her dreadful assignment in the drainage pit. I returned the broom, the dustpan and the full garbage bag to the guard, who had barely moved, thanked her and went back to my dorm, straight to the shower.

Chapter 16

Revelations

The scripture was an arrow—and I was the bull's eye, as I read Hosea 4:6, "My people are destroyed for lack of knowledge...." Those eight words changed my life from that moment on.

I noticed that the verse read, "My people are destroyed...." *His* people? *That's me!* I thought. What knowledge did I lack? I was a smart woman. What did I not know that had destroyed me in the past—or would destroy me in the future? I had always heard "what you don't know can't hurt you," but the Bible said it could, that it could *destroy* me—and I'd been destroyed long enough. Shocked, I realized that there had to be hidden spiritual dynamics behind my struggles, and I had to understand those invisible influences so that I could be healed and whole and free.

Immediately, the Holy Spirit began the process of revelation—giving supernatural understanding or "unveiling" of things a person could not perceive clearly without His help. He began to reveal why I had been destroyed all of my life, from the inside out, and why I had been unable to stop it. Over time, He gave me insight into the roots of some of my life-long struggles—with rejection and self-hatred, with alcohol, with the occult, with independence and rebellion— and allowed me to see them for what they really were: precision tools of the enemy of my soul.

There it was, the knowledge I lacked: not knowing that the devil was real and active and determined to "kill, steal and destroy" (John 10:10). And what had destroyed me for years was something I'd realized soon after I received the baptism of the Holy Spirit—that I did have an enemy, an invisible foe who was not less real or less active just because I couldn't see him.

One of the first threads this stealthy, subtle enemy began to weave into the fabric of my life was a constant sense of not belonging. Rejection hovered over me like a black cloud, and no matter how I tried I could never get out from under it. I could not remember a time I did not feel rejected, nor could I remember a specific traumatic event that triggered those feelings. I just knew that, despite the love of my family, I never felt like I fit in anywhere, with anyone.

Growing up, one of my closest friends was a tall, thin, blue-eyed blonde whose attractiveness drew attention and compliments everywhere she went. I, on the other hand, had dark eyes and dark, straight hair, which no one ever complimented, and was unnaturally overweight by the time I was ten or eleven years old. In the privacy of my mind, I constantly compared myself to my fair, slender friend, which only made me feel worse. In addition, other children teased me and joked about my weight with the kind of piercing meanness that can only be shot like a fiery dart from one child's mouth into another's heart. I began to hate myself and was soon convinced that no one liked me at all and that everyone else was rejecting me too. Whether or not people really were rejecting me, I believed they were—and because I believed it, it might as well have been the gospel truth.

In high school, I gained superficial acceptance because I often won contests or sporting events or science fairs, and because I had genuine leadership ability that the enemy often perverted and used to lead others into mischief. Even when I felt I did not fit in, I acted like I did and succeeded in fooling a large number of people. With my false confidence, I learned to sail through life like a guest at a masquerade party, changing my masks to fit whatever situation I was in—always miserable inside and never comfortable in my costume.

Being black-balled by the sorority in college reinforced my rejection in an incredibly painful way. But it was the rape that took rejection and shame to a whole new level—such degrees of trauma and anguish that only a miracle could truly heal me. The power behind so much of what I did was the fact that I was trying desperately to escape the torment of an event I had not planned and the deep, destructive impact of which I could not control. If rejection was a thread running through my life, being raped sewed me into a pocket of self-hatred and shame, which later I came to recognize as symptoms of rejection.

By the time I left college and entered the work world, I was an expert at making myself appear confident, happy and perfectly in control. But I did find myself unexplainably driven in my career. Performance had proven effective at camouflaging the way I felt about myself—at least to the undiscerning eye. But I knew better; it never made me feel the slightest bit affirmed by myself or by anyone else.

Always focused and diligent and willing to exert more effort than the next person, I became almost obsessed with my work, pushed by something more than the simple desire to excel in my job and earn a comfortable living. It was all a cover-up. Looking back from my prison cell as the Holy Spirit gave me revelation into how deeply and thoroughly feelings of rejection had affected my life, I realized that all of my efforts to perform and "do well" were nothing more than vain attempts to escape the pain that lived inside of me, which was impossible. I was doing everything I could to make my hurt go away—and failing miserably. I did not know it at the time, but came to see the truth about myself. I really had been diligent and smart and a hard worker, but the enemy had perverted those qualities and turned them into a workaholic compulsion fueled by the pain of my past.

As I began to accumulate money, I was trying to buy my way out of feeling rejected. I grew to understand that there is not a price tag on self-worth, that only the Lord can implant a true sense of value in a person. It was no wonder that, no matter how many expensive purchases I made, I still felt impotent on the inside; no matter how many exotic vacations I took, I could never run away from myself; no matter how many extravagant parties I hosted or attended, I still felt desperately alone; no matter how many beautiful clothes I wore, I was still revolted when I looked at myself. I finally understood why, no matter what I tried, I went to bed night after night with a throbbing ache in the bottom of my heart—the familiar feeling that I just was not "right."

Reflecting on my life, I realized that my feelings of rejection reached their apex, at least in terms of my response to them, soon after I purchased my home and hired a decorator to remodel the master bath. I allowed him to design the room and, although I knew his plans included covering all the walls with mirrors, I was not prepared for the impact this decorating technique would have on me. The poor self-image I had struggled with since childhood had grown up right along with me. Even though I had lost my excess weight, as a young professional woman I hated myself so much that I refused to turn on the lights when I entered my newly remodeled bathroom because the sight of myself was so repulsive to me. With mirrors mocking me from every wall, I could not keep from having to look at myself a hundred times as one reflection reflected another—and I was not someone I wanted to see.

By the time I got to prison and endured the harsh treatment of guards, the pervasive disregard for the value of inmates as real people with real feelings and the horror of strip searches, the enemy had woven rejection into my heart in such knots that it could not be untangled by any force less than the power of the Word and the Holy Spirit.

We continued our revelatory journey through my life, and as the Holy Spirit kept revealing more of the truth of my past to me, He showed me that drinking was one of the ways I coped with my raging rejection. I drank in order to feel socially acceptable and to experience the cheap, short-lived giddiness that results from too much alcohol. But He also showed me that my attraction to alcohol did not begin as a teenager or a college student, but as a small child. He revealed that alcohol had been wooing me all of my life and my desire for it had been hiding somewhere deep inside of me like a smoldering ember that burst into flame as soon as I was old enough to get my hands on it.

As a five-year-old little girl, playing at my grandparents' house one summer afternoon, I wandered into my grandfather's clothes closet. I flipped through his ties, ran my hands over the fabric of his suits and tried on his shoes, which were almost large enough to hold both of my little feet at the same time. And then my eyes locked onto the sight that lit the match inside of me—a sparkling, colorful display of liquor bottles perched on the top shelf of his closet. I stood gazing up at the bottles, wide-eyed with wonder, and knowing exactly what they were because I had seen women cooking with bourbon and various liqueurs—and they wouldn't let me taste them!

I knew I was not allowed to have anything that came out of a bottle like the ones on my grandfather's shelf, but the spark of a desire that would lie dormant for years was ignited in me that day. I was too short to reach the bottles, but oh, how I wanted them! Finally accepting the fact that they were out of my grasp, I turned and walked out of the closet with an unconscious determination tucked away in my five-year-old heart: *I'm going to get bottles like those someday.*

"Someday" came when I was about sixteen, and something inside of me never forgot the vow I had made years earlier. Once I had my driver's license, my mother allowed me to use her car almost any time I asked, so I often had the freedom to drive anywhere I wanted to go. Alcohol might have been beyond my reach at age five, but it was not when I was sixteen. Once again, I felt the unexplainable pull of an invisible force drawing me toward it. The problem was, like many counties in the American south, ours was a "dry county," which meant that the buying and selling of alcohol was illegal within the county limits. But the unseen power that pulled me toward alcohol also gave me the desire to make considerable effort to obtain it, which meant driving out into the country to the home of the local bootlegger—which I did frequently until I went to college.

Once in college, I had easy access to free-flowing liquor and was surrounded by people who were drinking—and that was like dumping gasoline on the fire that had already started burning in me. When I began my career, and until I went to prison, alcohol was a companion I continued to trust for relief despite its record as a miserable failure in my life for years.

Pulling my thoughts out of the past and into the present, I asked "Holy Spirit, what else? What else have I not understood about my life and my past? In what other areas has the lack of knowledge destroyed me?" As I prayed, He led me to consider my spiritual life.

From an early age, I had been interested in spiritual things, and my family had always attended church. Faithful to our local congregation, we were involved in every activity the church offered—from pancake breakfasts to potluck suppers, from Sunday school to softball teams—and everything in between. Even my Brownie troop met at the church!

Our church hosted a youth revival for several days during the summer when I was twelve years old. I had never heard such upbeat, happy music in church, and I found myself drawn to the music and impressed by the minister's obvious passion for the Lord. The people on the revival team were Christians, I knew. They loved God—*and they were having fun.* As I listened to the message that night and heard the preacher talk about being born again, I began to feel the weight of sin in my own heart. I wanted to know that my sins were forgiven, but it didn't hurt that I had observed Christians who were joyful and vibrant and full of life! Under the burden of my conviction, I walked down the aisle of the church one night and prayed to receive Jesus as my Savior.

I didn't really know what to do next, how to grow in my

newfound faith, so I continued going to church as often as possible and singing in the youth choir, but taking little responsibility for developing a personal relationship with the Lord. I did not understand how vital it was for me to immerse myself in the Word and allow it to shape my life.

Lack of knowledge of the Word, coupled with a genuine spiritual curiosity, allowed me to travel down the dangerous path into the occult, and the Holy Spirit showed me that I had taken my first steps at a much younger age than I realized. Like many American children, I received a popular fortune-telling game as a gift one Christmas and played with it often and innocently. As a young teenager, I had attended slumber parties where someone inevitably rallied a group of giggling girls around the cause of trying to levitate a person or an object. I also read my horoscope in newspapers and magazines, just because I was curious and believed in powers beyond natural knowledge. As a young adult, the New Age pursuits I found myself engaged in were simply the next step in my spiritual deception—a journey that started with something as simple as a board game.

The Holy Spirit showed me that my occult activities had all been a perverted effort to satisfy my spiritual longings. He gave me the understanding that I was made to connect with God, to be in relationship with Him and that everyone has an internal void that only He can fill. Because I did not know His Word, I did not know the difference between the dark side of the spiritual realm and the light side, so I tried to fill my emptiness with spiritual activities that were presented to me as good when in fact they were thoroughly evil and destructive. Before I knew who God really was, I didn't know who He was not! No wonder I stayed spiritually frustrated and always felt so disconnected and far from Him.

Wow! I could see how it all worked. Walking with the Holy Spirit through those areas of my past was like looking at an aerial photo of myself. Once I got far enough above it, I could easily discern how the enemy had made a not-so-pretty picture of my life. He had distorted the truth about me all of my life, but I now saw that the Lord had a beautiful picture, full of divine strategies and redemption. As He showed me who I really was underneath the ugliness the enemy had tried to impose by his schemes, I realized that I was not rejected; I was deeply loved and accepted by the Lord. But the enemy knew how powerful that understanding would be, so he attacked me from an early age. I also understood that I was created to be filled with the Holy Spirit, not with alcohol, which is often called "spirits," and to be influenced by Him and not to be under the influence of a drink. Furthermore, I came to see that I was made to love and worship the Lord and to walk in the power and victory of His Spirit, not to be seduced by false belief systems or their dark, demonic forces.

I continued to receive revelation about these issues, and the truth of both the enemy's perversion and of the Lord's redemption sprang to life in me: The truth *does* set us free. Once I knew the truth, I found freedom. I was still imprisoned physically, but I was able to take a quantum leap out of the shackles on my soul.

Chapter 17

An Upward Departure?

Prison was not a very private place, and I despised that. Mail call was one of the daily rituals during which I always longed for a few moments alone. It was good and bad at the same time. Outside of the opportunity to see family and friends during visiting hours, mail call provided us our most intimate contact with the world beyond prison walls and was usually a source of comfort for me because my mother was so faithful to write. Mike wrote occasionally, but most of our communication—which was happening less and less as our lives traveled separate paths—took place by telephone.

My heart broke every time I saw the same women leave mail call empty-handed day after day. When I shared that with my mother, I also gave her the names and I.D. numbers of a few of those women, and within several days they had mail because she sent them cheerful little notes and daily devotional books from her church.

I never enjoyed living "in a fishbowl," especially being deprived of seemingly insignificant personal moments like reading a letter without an audience. Whenever I received anything that appeared official or bore my attorney's return address, I definitely did not want to read it in front of on-lookers, even though I knew that every piece of mail handed out had already been opened and read by prison officials, and that my news was only "new" to me.

One March afternoon in 1994, I received a letter from my attorney. Anticipating an update on my appeal, I knew that this was a perfect opportunity for the Lord to perform the miracle for which I'd been longing—an early release. If He took that opportunity, then within minutes I would finally be reading the news I was so desperate to hear. Even though I was overwhelmed by thoughts of my possible release, I held myself together as I tried to make a speedy, inconspicuous exit from the mail call area. I headed for the privacy of the bathroom, which had become the refuge to which I retreated any time I wanted to be by myself. I locked the door of the stall behind me, and quickly skimmed the document, looking eagerly for the words "conviction overturned," followed by the confirmation that I would soon be on my way home.

I read instead, "However, the court does have authority to grant an upward departure [an extension of my prison term] where the facts warrant such action. This is so in your case . . ." No! It could not be! I read the letter again, certain I had misunderstood that horrible report. But I had not; I had read it correctly the first time. My appeal had been heard in the federal court of appeals in New Orleans and had not been decided in my favor.

I was not getting out of prison anytime soon.

What was worse, Judge Faulk could re-sentence me and order me to stay locked up even longer! I sat alone with my letter in the bathroom stall, stunned, with another hope shattered. I wanted to fall apart.

Sinking to a brand-new level of desperation, I whispered, "Holy Spirit, You have *got* to help me," and I meant it from the core of my being. Without a measure of grace and strength I had not experienced before, there was no way I could endure the days ahead, not knowing whether the judge would give me more time. I had discovered that God never runs out; there was always more of Him when I needed more— and I had never needed more of Him than at that moment.

I thought I had trusted the Lord before, but this news thrust me into a crossroads at which I had to choose afresh to let go of my life and my future, placing everything in His hands with a deeper surrender than ever. I had to choose to believe that my situation was perfectly under His watchful eye and loving control, even though I had no idea what lay ahead of me.

I knew I could not stay in the bathroom all afternoon, but at that moment I wanted to sit and hide in that stall for the rest of my life. I was devastated, but I *had* to go back to my cell, and I wanted to do so with as much composure as I could muster. My painful disappointment was private, and I wanted to keep it that way. I knew that an emotional release would not affect my circumstances in the least and certainly would not help me. Knowing I could not allow myself to break down, I took a deep breath, rounded up my emotions headed back toward my bunk as if nothing had happened.

But something *had* happened, and I could not ignore it in my heart or in my mind. I had intentionally created too much distance between myself and my old familiar den of denial to start crawling back into it. I had already dealt with the devastation of not being pardoned, and now I had to wrestle with the idea that my prison term could be lengthened. Thoughts of an extended stay at Benton threatened to pin me to the mat. I had already learned that dwelling on unpleasant possibilities or trying to figure out the future would only defeat me. I had to find a way to push back my "what-if" wonderings, to pick myself up and go on the offensive against them. It was a tough match, part of which I fought and began to win in the arena of my journal:

> *3/13/94: I am separated, but then there is mail call. I am apart, but then there is a phone. For an instant, I thought of the distance between my family and me. Yet they have never turned their backs on me—not once. How did the Father feel knowing He had to turn His back on sin— knowing the pain and suffering His Son would encounter? I am apart, separated, but I know He loves me. I know.*

The victory of knowing the Lord loved me, once apprehended, then had to be guarded. For the next few weeks I did not share my news; instead, I lived each day with a quiet but fierce resolve to maintain the triumph over my latest challenge. I remembered again one of the first foundational truths I learned on my spiritual journey, that there were two kingdoms at war—satan's kingdom of darkness and God's Kingdom of light—and they were fighting over me! The kingdom of darkness had once again launched an attack against its favorite combat zone—my mind.

As the Holy Spirit gave me understanding of the battle raging over me, He also taught me how to stand against the enemy's mental assaults. The first weapon He gave me came from the arsenal of the Word, from Philippians 4:8. When I read it, I saw my marching orders: "Whatever things are true, whatever things are noble, whatever things are just, whatever things are pure, whatever things are lovely, whatever things are of good report, if there is any virtue and if there is anything praiseworthy—meditate on these things."

The command was clear: I could only think thoughts that fit into one of those eight categories. If a thought did not pass the "Philippians 4:8 test," I could not allow myself to think it. Perhaps those standards of the Holy Spirit seemed extreme, but I lived in an extreme situation. Prison had a way of multiplying every defeat, and I knew that if I surrendered in the battle for my mind, I would lose the war for my life.

Day by day, sometimes even moment by moment, I had to enforce the Holy Spirit's categories in my mind. I had to do as Deuteronomy 30:19 instructed, to "choose life," and I had to start by quickly rejecting every negative thought, every lie of the enemy. How did I know what the lies of the enemy were? I could only recognize the lies by knowing the truth. Many times, a fiery dart of hopelessness would fly from the pit of hell, carrying a message to my mind and causing me to think thoughts such as, *I could be here another five years* or, worse, *I may never get out of this place.* I had to deflect that dart before its message was embedded in my mind, and the Holy Spirit faithfully reminded me of truths that would accomplish that purpose. To shoot down a thought like, *You may never get out of here,* I would personalize a Bible verse like Jeremiah 29:11 and respond by thinking, *God has plans for me—plans for good and not for evil, plans to give me a future and hope!*

In the midst of terrible uncertainty, I had to choose to keep my mind on the truth of God's love and His promises of good plans for my future. Those were extremely difficult "basic training" days, but the lessons I learned about fighting the battles of the mind were some of the most critical instructions I ever received and were principles that set me on a path of increasing victory and freedom.

In the weeks and months preceding the letter from my attorney, the Holy Spirit had already been teaching me about the mind. He knew what was coming, so He prepared me. I had been learning that people are three-part beings: spirit, soul and body, and that the soul includes the mind, the will and the emotions. Given that definition, I had been living from my soul all my life! That was terrible! I needed to be living from my spirit—and the possibility of increased prison time gave me the ideal chance to put that recent understanding into practice.

I had choices to make: faith or fear, peace or panic. I could let my mind wander and ask myself all kinds of questions, such as "What if I get more time?" Or, I could keep my thoughts on a short leash and think things like, *Because the Lord loves me, His timing for my life is absolutely perfect.*

I pulled on Him with everything in me, just for the strength to survive every day with my sanity intact. I did everything I could do to stay strong on my own but I knew the prayers of other people were essential reinforcements in the battle, so I told a few of the women in the Remnant Group what had happened, knowing they would pray. As difficult as it had been for me in the past to admit my need for others, I had to admit again that, yes, I really needed my friends.

Easter was approaching and it was early that year. Would I be able to celebrate in the midst of my internal struggles? Yes. I could not imagine any circumstance so horrible—even the possibility of spending more time behind bars—that it would prohibit my rejoicing Jesus' victory. After all, He had shared His victory with me, and it had completely changed me. I was determined to celebrate Easter, and I did. That night, I reflected on my second Easter Sunday at Benton:

4/3/94: Easter in prison, yet free! I would never have guessed this course for my life, yet would I have ever found peace? Probably not. Just to be in His presence. Funny, you know you are comfortable with someone when you can sit quietly—no words exchanged—and are content, happy. Today I had that need—just to be with Him.

The week after Easter, I was required to attend a class to learn how to operate a buffer properly, because I was being trained to buff floors as part of my job in the dorm. On my way to class that morning, a guard stopped me and said, "Hey, Forsythe. Pack out."

I was shocked. *Where are they sending me?* I wondered. The guard was telling me to go back to my cell and pack my clothes and my few belongings. I would have to turn in my prison uniform and change into my civilian clothes. One thing was sure: I was leaving. But where was I going? I had seen so many other inmates go through these same motions and never come back to Benton. Was it finally my turn? Was I being released after all?

I found myself once again face-to-face with another maddening unknown of prison life: no one would tell me what was about to happen. With a strange mixture of dread over what might take place and hope that I could be released, I quickly inventoried my possessions, all of which fit into two small boxes. I wondered if I would ever see them again and, if so, under what circumstances. I changed into my civilian clothes and went to the laundry room to turn in my linens and my uniforms. Then I took a walk of uncertainty that seemed as if it would last forever, hoping every step was getting me closer to freedom, but knowing it could be leading anywhere.

After I arrived at the R and D building, an officer processed my paperwork, stored my belongings in a closet and put me in the same holding cell I had been in on the day I arrived. But this time I was different. This time, I was there having met the Holy Spirit in a personal and powerful way. I was free from the demonic influences that had tormented me before. I had been learning to hear the Holy Spirit's voice and to trust Him. This time, peace surrounded me in an unbelievable way. Standing in that cell, not knowing what was about to happen to me, I found myself trusting Him for everything I did not know.

Of course, I was hoping I had packed out because something had changed and I was being released. I asked myself again, *Could it be?* At the same time, I knew that the remarkable, pervading sense of peace that filled my heart was unusual and wondered why I needed it. The Holy Spirit knew. He knew what I was about to encounter. And He gave me His peace because I was about to experience something so awful that only He—*only He*—could shelter me, sustain me and enable me to survive.

Chapter 18

In Transit

"Forsythe, put your legs closer together." This was it—my most humiliating moment yet, outside of the strip searches. Just when I thought I had experienced almost every possible manifestation of shame, I found myself subjected to the new and unique horror of being handcuffed and shackled. The feel of those cold, heavy metal bands around my wrists and ankles made me shudder all the way to my bones. The shame and reproach from which I thought I had been healed came flooding back to me as if I were standing in the ocean, over-come by a wave from behind.

Two U.S. Marshals, one male and one female, had arrived while I was waiting in the holding cell. Through the glass wall, I had been able to see them talking with the guards and assumed they were there for me. But that assumption had not been able to prevent the bolt of terror that shot through me and shattered my peace when they opened the door of the cell and snapped, "Forsythe! Get out here!" They had come to take me away, in chains, with nothing but the clothes I was wearing—and they would not tell me where I was going.

The Marshals took me by the arms, one on each side, and led my slow, stiff, frightened self out of the R and D building. This was not the kind of exit I had hoped to make from Benton. In fact, I had never been more afraid in my entire life than I was during those few moments, and they set the tone for everything else I would encounter that day. Scared and embarrassed to the core of my being, I shuffled my shackled feet awkwardly toward the Marshals' police car and stumbled into the back seat, behind a metal security grid. Obviously, I was going to be "in transit." I was being moved somewhere, and hoped it was somewhere nearby. I had heard stories about the unspeakable things that sometimes happened to inmates while they were in transit, and I prayed that we would arrive without incident.

Once the Marshals got into the car, I hoped they would give me some sort of indication as to where they might be taking me. But when I asked, the only answer they ever gave was an annoyed-sounding: "We can't tell you anything." So I did not have any idea where we were going or how long it would take to get there.

After about an hour's drive, with me still in handcuffs and shackles, the Marshals decided to stop for lunch. I wanted—and needed—a chance to visit a restroom, but they would not remove the handcuffs or the shackles in order for me to go inside the restaurant, so I chose to stay in the car. I could not imagine anything more degrading than having to walk through a public place in chains. Because they were not allowed to leave me alone in the car, one of the Marshals went into the restaurant while the other one kept watch over me. I hoped our destination was not much farther, but of course, I did not know. The entire experience was minute-by-minute torture.

When we resumed our journey, I looked out my backseat window as the car traveled down a state highway I did not recognize and saw the most incredible sight: hundreds of glorious Texas bluebonnets in the median of the divided road. God had broken through! Those flowers were His billboard to me. I knew that He had allowed me to see something beautiful just to assure me of His presence and His love and His complete knowledge of my nightmare of a day. They were His "Mary, I'm with you" message to me, and seeing them brought me comfort and a sense of closeness to Him that was beyond the ability of any ordinary bluebonnet!

I was thoroughly convinced that He did know, that He did care, that He did want me to hold on, and that truly, He was with me. He had not failed me; He had not forsaken me; and clearly, He and I were about to face new challenges together. And I knew that, whatever they were, I could not go through them without Him.

I thought about a story I had recently read in Corrie ten Boom's book *Tramp for the Lord*. She had experienced her own invasion of grace not in the form of a flower, but in an equally dramatic way, when she was imprisoned during World War II at the dreaded German concentration camp, Ravensbruck.

Roll call sometimes lasted three hours and every day the sun rose a little later and the icy-cold wind blew a little stronger. Standing in the gray of the dawn I would try to repeat, through shivering lips, that verse of Scripture which had come to mean so much to me: "Who shall separate us from the love of Christ? Shall tribulation, or distress, or persecution, or famine, or nakedness, or peril, or sword? As it is written, for thy sake we are killed all the day long;

we are accounted as sheep for the slaughter" (Romans 8:35, 36). In all this there was an overwhelming victory through Jesus who has proved His love for me by dying on the cross. But there came a time when repeating the words did not help. I needed more. "Oh God," I prayed, "reveal Yourself somehow."

Then one morning the woman directly in front of me sank to the ground. In a moment a young woman guard was standing over her, a whip in her hand.

"Get up," she screamed in a rage. "How dare you think you can lie down when everyone else is standing!"

I could hardly bear to see what was happening in front of me. Surely this is the end of us all, *I thought. Then suddenly a skylark started to sing high in the sky. The sweet, pure notes of the bird rose on the still cold air. Every head turned upward, away from the carnage before us, listening to the sound of the skylark soaring over the crematorium. The words of the psalmist ran through my mind: "For as the heaven is high above the earth, so great is [God's] mercy toward them that fear Him" (Psalms 103:11).*

There in that prison I saw things from God's point of view. The reality of God's love was just as sure as the cruelty of men.

O love of God, how deep and great, far deeper than man's deepest hate.

Every morning for the next three weeks, just at the time of roll call, the skylark appeared. In his sweet song I heard the call of God to turn my eyes away from the cruelty of men to the ocean of God's love.[1]

Corrie had a skylark; I had a field of bluebonnets; and both were tangible evidence of the Lord's watchful eye and listening ear inclined toward a daughter who desperately needed to know her Father was near. I knew my destination could not possibly be as horrible as Ravensbruck and hoped that wherever I was going would not be nearly as cruel as I feared it could be.

Before much longer, we pulled into a driveway that led to a strange-looking building—strange because it did not have any windows, not one. All I saw was one word on a sign: "Ashfield." No wonder I had been terrified. I had heard of Ashfield—and the stories were not good. Even the outside of the building looked harsh. All I could do was hope that I would not be in this cold, lifeless maximum-security holding facility for long.

When the Marshals ordered, "Forsythe, get out," and took me inside the building, I felt as though I had just stepped into hell itself. I was stunned, but did not say a word. Just the thought that I might have to stay in this hideous place was incomprehensible to me; I did not think I could bear it. Everything about that prison was cruel. Suddenly, being in the Marshals' custody became much more appealing; I would have willingly gotten back into their car just to go somewhere else—*anywhere* would have been better than Ashfield. *Surely they are not leaving me here,* I thought. But they were.

The very atmosphere of Ashfield seemed to drip with evil. I did not know it was possible for human beings to be as cold, as tough, or as mean-spirited as those guards were. One of the first things I was ordered to do was to follow a female guard into a shower area, where she instructed me to strip and to wash my hair and my body with a foul-smelling shampoo intended to kill lice. Loss of privacy took on a whole new meaning to me that day as I showered in front of an audience.

After the shower, as I stood totally naked, the guard grabbed my bra and cut the underwire out of it before tossing it back to me. Thoroughly humiliated, I dressed myself in the dirty orange jumpsuit I had been issued and put on the shoes they gave me: two plastic flip-flops, both for the left foot. I then followed a male guard into a room where he instructed me to grab a mattress, but the mattresses did not look like any mattresses I had ever seen. They were smelly and lumpy and heavy and covered with stains I could not identify.

With the guard, I lumbered down a cold, gray hallway dragging my mattress, assuming he was taking me to a cell. The women's cellblock was at the end of a long dingy corridor, past the men's block where the male inmates peered greedily through the steel bars on their locked doors. I was certain they would have attacked me had the bars not restrained them. I felt like every demon in hell was mocking and taunting and cursing me as I passed the men screaming obscenities, calling me names and making noises my ears had never heard before.

"Just keep looking straight ahead," was the guard's only instruction. I was terrified to look anywhere else. When one unruly eye did just barely glance in the direction of the cells, I caught a glimpse of some of the men and thought, *These people are like animals. I cannot believe they are even human.*

We were approaching the end of the hall, where the women were kept. Just a few more steps and I would arrive at the tiny, musty configuration of bars and walls that would be my cell for I-didn't-know-how-long. I had already been there too long for my comfort, and my stay had just begun. Already, I was wondering, *Am I going to end up like these people? Will this place turn me into something inhuman too?*

In the short time I had been in this dungeon called Ashfield, I had seen enough to know that I could not find one shred of human dignity there. But I also knew that if I could find God there, I could find Him anywhere.

Why have they sent me here? I wondered. *And what on earth will the Lord do with me in this seemingly God-forsaken place?*

Chapter 19

A Remnant Everywhere

As the guard led me to my cell, one of eight individual rooms with heavy doors and locks in a small dimly-lit cellblock (or "tank") behind two security doors, I remembered Corrie ten Boom once again. Although she was held captive in another time and in another country, I knew that she must have experienced some of the same things I was experiencing. After all, pain is universal, fear is universal, and despair is universal. But so is the love of God, and I knew that He was able to help me just as He had helped her.

I stood in my cell and could hardly believe how horrible Ashfield was. Surrounded by the tangible blackness, I wondered how people could actually survive in these conditions. At the same time, I understood why the people there looked so totally empty, hopeless and tormented. Everyone I saw was depressed.

The strange thing was that, as abysmal as Ashfield was, I knew deep in my heart that the Holy Spirit had prepared me to be there. In every way, He had provided the spiritual preparation I needed to endure those unspeakably awful conditions.

So there we were, just the Holy Spirit and me, in the most wretched environment imaginable.

I thought of the story Corrie ten Boom told about arriving at the Ravensbruck to find the barracks teeming with fleas. Her sister, Betsie, had reminded her of a Bible passage they had recently read, 1 Thessalonians 5:16-18, "Rejoice always, pray without ceasing, in everything give thanks; for this is the will of God in Christ Jesus for you." They obeyed His Word and gave thanks to the Lord, even for the fleas. They realized that the fleas kept the guards away so that they could read the Bible and share hope with the other women in their barracks! If they could be thankful in their situation, I could be thankful in mine. I would remember that even in a place like Ashfield, He was there. I would talk to Him; I would listen to Him and obey; and I would survive because He was there. Perhaps the place was unfit for human life, but God didn't seem to mind; He was still there.

I was grateful for the strength I gained by remembering Corrie, but had to call my thoughts back to the present moment. I did not know what time it was, but I did know that I was hungry and that no one else was eating. I was relieved when a guard finally brought me a tray of food.

Outside my cell was a small common area that contained two steel tables where the inmates ate their meals. There was no chow hall at Ashfield, so meals were shoved through horizontal slats in the security doors. I sat down at a steel table and looked at my unidentifiable dinner. The term "mystery meat" took on a whole new meaning! Nevertheless, whatever was before me was something God had provided, so I bowed my head and thanked Him for it, saying, "Lord, thank You for this food. I don't really know what it is, but I am trusting You to use it to strengthen me."

After I had eaten, I went back to my cell. What would I do next? More trapped than ever, I had two options: sit on the bunk and look at the walls or lie on the bunk and look at the ceiling. The cell contained nothing but a flimsy little bed, a tiny sink and a cold stainless steel toilet beside the door. Through the bars, the toilet was in plain view of anyone who wanted to see it or the person using it. I was disgusted.

Hundreds of scratches marred the ceiling where previous inmates had stood on the bed attempting to smooth their broken fingernails on its roughness. People's bodies seemed to deteriorate at Ashfield in a way I had not observed anywhere else. *How is it possible that human life looks so lifeless?* I wondered. Skin became dry and scaly and blotchy; fingernails broke; hair fell out. Almost immediately after my arrival, these unpleasant transformations began happening to me. This place was so dark and deathly that it was impossible for most healthy physical functions to continue within its walls.

I could not focus on the degradation, though. I could not allow myself to think about how thoroughly dismal Ashfield was. I needed to reel in my thoughts and round up my sensibilities so that I could begin to exist in that environment.

Scared and skeptical that I would find anything I would consider livable, I continued to investigate my new surroundings. I saw that, in addition to the two tables, the cellblock included two tiny showers with thin, worn plastic curtains in a small room. Everything about those showers was nasty. I could not imagine how they could be so filthy because I could tell someone had been cleaning them. I nearly gagged when I walked in and breathed the pungent odor of institutional disinfectant. I asked no one, *How can this place be so gross when it reeks of cleaning fluid?*

I soon found out that the inmates in the block took turns cleaning the showers once a day, and that the suffocating smell of disinfectant just hung in the air day after day because there was no apparent air circulation. We certainly did not have the option to open a window and ventilate the place!

If the stench were not enough, there was no way to escape the almost inhuman sounds that ricocheted around the prison halls. The women's tank was close to "the hole," the most dreaded place in any prison, the cells that were used for solitary confinement. The screaming and moaning and wailing and animal-like sounds that came from the hole were enough to push a person into insanity—and often did. They were sounds I had never heard before, too hideous to be accurately described.

Before lockdown that first night, a young woman named Rita showed up at my cell door. She looked like someone who had been living for quite a while in the conditions I had just surveyed—stringy hair, empty eyes and a complexion the color of paste. "Are you a Christian?" she asked. She had seen me bow my head before I ate and assumed I was praying.

"Yes, I am," I responded. A grin spread across her face, revealing the fact that she had no front teeth, as she told me that she had prayed just the night before and asked the Lord to send her someone who could teach the Bible. With the confidence that only comes from answered prayer, she invited me to her cell, and asked, "What do you need?"

I said, "Rita, I don't have anything. They didn't let me bring *anything*."

"Don't worry," she said, "I have everything you need."

I was amazed by her generosity. The first thing I wanted to do was to brush my teeth, and Rita offered me a drop of toothpaste so that I could brush them with my finger. After that she handed me her Bible. This was the moment she had asked the Lord for. We sat down on the concrete floor together and began to talk. Soon a young Spanish woman joined us and stayed while I shared, despite the fact that she spoke very little English. Even though she did not understand much, maybe she simply sensed the presence of the Lord and did not want to leave. Corrie ten Boom was right: "…in darkness God's truth shines most clear."[2] We were in a dark place all right, but that night the darkness fled as the truth of God's Word invaded that jail cell.

By the time I heard the guard's voice announce over the P.A. system, "Five minutes 'til lockdown," I was exhausted and filled with uncertainty, yet strangely at peace. There I was, standing in a maximum security prison, without even a toothbrush to my name, but knowing that the Lord had heard Rita's prayer.

I had a prayer of my own. I needed a Bible. Getting one didn't seem possible, but I asked the Lord for one anyway, and He brought me unexpected provision from a most unlikely source. One of the most hardened women at Ashfield was Tonya. She looked tough, thought tough, acted tough and talked tough. To my utter amazement, she walked up to me on my second day there and grunted, "Here. Thought you might want this." I looked down and saw that she was giving me a Bible—the one thing I really needed! *You never change,* I spoke silently to the Lord, *You were my provider at Benton, and You're my provider in this place. You still know exactly what I need.*

And I needed a lot at Ashfield. I needed a lot of grace and patience and inner peace just to live through the realities of its harsh physical environment. All of the lights in the prison were fluorescent and their intensity produced an excessive, eerie brightness. The cinder block walls were painted a dark steely gray, so when the lights were on, a strange glare hovered over the entire place. The lights were on a timer, and perhaps just to increase the challenge of incarceration, they were only off from about 1:00 in the morning until about 5:00, making deep or restful sleep virtually impossible.

On top of that, after every meal, we had to beat our trays against the edge of the garbage containers to remove all of the uneaten food before we sent them to the dish room. That repeated banging three times a day was one of the most obnoxious sounds I had ever heard, and every slam of a tray was loaded with rage and rebellion.

The television that hung from the wall of the common area blared constantly and was usually tuned to something violent or vulgar. I supposed that most of the inmates had heard so many angry words and crashes and gunshots in their lives that those offensive programs did not bother them. Or perhaps they had just been there so long that they did not even notice.

On one occasion, I was almost at my wits' end with the incessant racket of the television. I said to the Lord, "Lord, I just can't take the noise. Could You please just get something decent on this television?" The next thing I knew, a family movie appeared on the screen—a relief to my ears and a reminder to my heart that He knew.

I did not know how long I would have to stay at Ashfield and quickly lost all sense of time while I was there. I knew I would not be there forever and that I had to maintain the inner life and internal standards I had developed at Benton. Corrie ten Boom said that the worst cancer in prison is selfishness, and I knew I could not turn inward or focus on myself even amid the horrors of a maximum-security facility.

The Holy Spirit had trained me to look beyond my own needs, see the needs of others and try to meet them. As I did, He met me. He had so precisely prepared me for the opportunities He would give me to serve in that dark place.

The Spirit quickly showed me practical ways to help the people around me. Every few days, the inmates were allowed to go outside for a short recreation time and some fresh air. The women were so lethargic and depressed that they rarely took advantage of the opportunity. Some of them had not been outside in a year or longer, being held captive in their captivity to the point that some seemed to forget they were really alive. I could not imagine it, but it was true. They had stayed inside so long that their skin had turned a pale shade of gray, and they had no muscle tone and no energy. I was able to inspire a few of these women to exercise, and if the Spirit had not helped me to accomplish anything else, encouraging them to begin to value themselves would have been enough.

At Ashfield, what we called "outside" was actually a fenced area of about 100 square feet with a concrete floor and a black tarpaulin as its roof. Even the fences along its sides had tarpaulins over them, so we could never see the sky even though we were technically outside. *At least there's fresh air,* I thought, *and at least it circulates.*

As I led a few inmates in some elementary exercise classes, I decided to set a personal goal of walking a mile per day and invited any of the women who were also interested to join me. Because we had no way to know how many laps around the fenced area would make a mile, I made a collect call to my parents and asked them to find out approximately how many average-sized human feet were in one mile. (I assumed my feet were about "average"!)

If I knew that, I reasoned, I could figure out how many laps it would take and could present that goal to the other women. My parents had the answer the next time I spoke with them by phone, and the Ashfield walking regimen was underway.

I could easily discern the hand of the Lord at work in the lives of some of the women, but He totally surprised me in the case of an eighteen-year-old inmate named Lori. The time I spent sharing the Word with Rita quickly grew into a daily Bible study. When we focused on God's promises together, our darkness felt lighter and our bondage less oppressive. We also began to take communion together, using water for wine and a small piece of bread we saved from our meal trays.

One night, I began to tell the women how I had asked Jesus into my heart when I was twelve years old. A young Catholic woman named Leticia had been in church all of her life, just as I had. She told me that she did not like to go to confession, but that she did want to talk to Jesus.

"I never heard of 'asking Jesus into your heart,'" she said. "Why would you do that?"

"When you ask Jesus to come into your heart as Lord and Savior and forgive you of your sins, you are born again."

"How do you do that?"

"I can lead you in a prayer."

She wanted to pray right then, so I said, "Just repeat after me: 'Father, I need Your help. I ask You to forgive me of my sins. Jesus, I believe that You died on the cross and rose again to save me. Come into my heart and teach me to hear Your voice. In Jesus' Name, Amen.'"

The women in that cell were not the only ones listening as Leticia gave her life to Jesus. Lori never came into the cell while we were having Bible study, but lingered in the common area close to the door and listened. One morning I was awakened about 3:00 A.M. by the sound of someone rattling the bars on my cell and whispering urgently, "Mary! Mary!" I awoke instantly and saw Lori. A guard had just told her to pack out because she was going to be in transit. Then she said, "I prayed last night, and I asked Jesus into my heart!"

Lori had heard me telling Leticia how to be born again, and had asked Jesus to be her Lord and Savior too. With tears in my eyes, I reached through the food slat in my door and took her hands in mine. I prayed for her, asking the Lord to watch over her and protect her and bless her and continue to reveal Himself to her. I never saw her again after that early morning announcement, but her salvation was another incredible opportunity to see the Lord's hand moving at Ashfield.

My days there reminded me of the famous opening line of Charles Dickens' novel, *A Tale of Two Cities*: "It was the best of times, it was the worst of times..." That was so true. I saw the Holy Spirit do amazing things, things perhaps I would not have seen if the circumstances had not been so unbearable. Ashfield was so evil and so lonely, but surely and steadily, the Holy Spirit breathed grace into the wretchedness and kept me from snapping emotionally or collapsing physically.

He preserved my mind so that I did not go insane in an environment where that could have easily happened. He helped me choose not to be bitter even though my circumstances were dreadful. He showed me that He has a remnant everywhere. Even at a maximum-security prison, in the midst of all the hard hearts, He had a handful of His people. His love was the force that enabled me to overcome the constant tendencies to be selfish. Corrie ten Boom had written, and I firmly believed that, "...stony indifference to others...was the most fatal disease" of the prison.[3]

I did not understand why I had been sent to Ashfield. I simply did what I knew to do to follow the Spirit by asking Him, almost without ceasing, "Lord, where are You at this moment?" And moment by moment, He carried me through those days.

I came to understand one of the last things Betsie ten Boom ever said to Corrie: "...there is no pit so deep that He is not deeper still."[4] Ashfield was a pit indeed, a seemingly endless abyss of darkness and despair. But Betsie was right: He was deeper still. *My* God, *my* Father, was deeper still.

It did not matter what else I had to experience at Ashfield or where I would have to go from there because the Holy Spirit had burned a word in my heart: "For I am persuaded that neither death nor life, nor angels nor principalities nor powers, nor things present nor things to come, nor height nor depth, nor any other created thing, shall be able to separate us from the love of God which is in Christ Jesus our Lord" (Romans 8:38, 39).

Even at Ashfield, nothing could separate me. Nothing.

Chapter 20

A Captive Audience

"Forsythe! Get up!" The guard's words were as sharp and rapid as machine gun fire as he startled me from a restless sleep. It was 4:30 in the morning at Ashfield. Groggily, I fumbled my way off of my bunk and waited for someone to let me know what was happening. Before too long, I was chained and shackled and led to a hallway where I stood until 7:00 A.M., waiting and wondering where I was going.

Two federal Marshals came and escorted me to a white government van, the kind so often used to transport groups of inmates. I was going to court. It was time for the re-sentencing hearing my attorney had written me about. Some women at Ashfield had been waiting a year or more for their court dates, so it seemed to be a miracle that mine had come after only several days. As we walked out of the building toward the van, I caught a glimpse of another one of God's billboards to me—the most glorious sunrise I had ever seen. A ball of brilliant red April sun was making its gentle climb over the horizon. I was somber; I was scared; but I was silently grateful for the chance to see a sliver of beauty in the midst of horrendous circumstances.

I climbed into the van with eight male inmates—all of us shackled and chained—who were also scheduled for court appearances that day and who persuaded the driver to turn on the radio and play the music loud enough to be heard outside. I just wanted to be still; I just wanted to be quiet.

A tall, lean man named Kenny sat beside me and began talking immediately. I paid little attention to him and muttered a half-hearted, "Well, praise the Lord," when he paused in such a way that I knew he was awaiting some kind of a response from me.

"Are you a Christian?" he asked, brimming with enthusiasm.

"Yes," I responded, still not wanting to interact with anyone.

"God has sent me an angel! I prayed last night that He would send someone to explain the book of Job to me." He pronounced that biblical book's name as if he were referring to an occupation—a job. I still didn't really want to talk, but my heart was softened by his hunger for truth, so Kenny asked me questions, and we had a Bible study right there in the van on our way to court! The guards and other inmates in the van were listening, but they did not intimidate me. They even turned down the radio, and I believed the Holy Spirit was speaking to them, as well as to Kenny.

With accusations of kidnapping and attempted murder stacked against him, Kenny's future did not look bright. For months he had been consumed by hopelessness, but the short time we spent focusing on the Word encouraged and strengthened both of us before we arrived at our destination. I knew that the Lord had graciously and supernaturally touched me because in my natural condition, I felt just inches away from complete physical and emotional collapse.

My eyes soon fell upon a familiar sight: the Earl Campbell Federal Building in downtown Dallas. So many times I had left my Highland Park home and driven to this building in my expensive sports car. So many times I had walked through its front door wearing the latest designer clothes. I had been here with high-priced attorneys whose fees I had the money to pay and who joined me for drinks after our meetings. I had been here with my head held high, confident that the legal challenges I faced would be nothing more than a speed bump on the road of my life. How proud I had been! How arrogant! And how mistaken.

This time, I had come to the Earl Campbell building as a federal prisoner. I had ridden in a government van and was escorted by armed guards. I entered through the back door and rode the service elevator to the floor where the holding tanks were. My hair was falling out; my fingernails were splitting and jagged; and my face was pale and blotchy. I was wearing an old orange jumpsuit and a pair of flip-flops that were both for the left foot. I had not been allowed to wear my glasses, but I did not need them in order to see how much everything—truly everything—had changed.

A guard led me to a holding tank and locked me in it. After a little while my attorney, Brad, visited me, and I knew by the look on his face that my appearance had left him struggling for words. I had not seen him since I had gone to Benton. I looked worse than ever—almost frightening—on the outside, but the Lord had done such a wonderful work inside of me that even he could tell. I shared with him how faithful the Lord had been to me and even prayed for him.

After Brad left, I was empty—completely drained and alone in the holding tank. I had never experienced such thorough physical and emotional exhaustion. While at Ashfield, I had neither slept nor eaten much, which resulted in a weakness and fatigue that I had never before experienced. In that condition, I realized that I had never stood in a place of such uncertainty concerning what the future held. I did not know what was about to happen to me, but I had to resist the fear that threatened to overwhelm me.

At that moment, the Holy Spirit whispered to me and said, "Praise Me." He asked me to walk around that holding tank with my hands raised, giving Him praise.

"No way," I said to Him in my heart. "I can't. I'm just too weak." After all, I needed every ounce of strength I had left to simply walk to the courtroom. I certainly was not physically able to lift my hands to worship the Lord.

But the Holy Spirit would not allow me to focus on my weaknesses. His prompting would not stop, and He began to remind me of various times at Benton when He had asked me to "praise my way through" other challenges and disappointments, using the weapon of worship as my way to victory. But I had never been as weak as I was that day. Praising Him was a choice, an act of my will, not something I *felt* like doing. *Will it make any difference?* I wondered—and realized I would never know unless I tried.

As I shuffled around the cell and began to hum softly, my focus slowly began to shift from the degradation of my captivity to the faithfulness of the Lord. Regardless of my circumstances, He was still faithful. I finally began to sing.

Although I was not much of a singer, I had always been one to make a joyful noise! But the Holy Spirit touched my voice that day and the sound was beautiful. Eventually, I was able to raise my hands in thanksgiving. Within minutes, the heavy oppression began to lift from me. Hope returned and peace began to fill my heart as the Holy Spirit released to me a life source I'd never drawn from before.

The men who had ridden to Dallas from Ashfield with me were all together in the holding tank next to mine. They could hear my singing and one of them yelled, "Mary, do you really believe God will forgive a murderer?" I knew they were all listening for the answer and realized that God had provided a captive audience! Around the cinder block walls, I shared the gospel with a man I could not see, a man the Lord had had His eye on and been pursuing for a long time. It was like a full-blown evangelistic crusade—only the preacher and the audience were all behind bars!

By the time the guards came and handcuffed and shackled me to take me into the courtroom, I was filled with the strength of God's presence and the peace that accompanied the assurance that my future was in His hands. As I entered the courtroom, I was painfully aware of all the people who were staring at me even though I could not see them clearly without my glasses. Some of those people I had known before I went to prison, like my sister and my accountant, and I knew that they were astonished by the way I looked.

Even with only my naturally poor eyesight, I could depict a familiar face on the bench—Judge John Faulk. The team of prosecutors from my trial was also there and seemed glad to have an opportunity to punish me again. The intensity of their disdain for me was palpable, and it had not lessened since the last time we were on opposing sides in a courtroom.

The hearing was brief, no longer than fifteen minutes. The judge asked the prosecuting attorney if she wanted an upward departure or if she suggested that my original sentence stand. I held my breath as the legal parties spoke about my future as if I were not even present. Throughout the entire surreal experience, I felt as though I were in the studio audience of a courtroom drama—only I was the main character! Did they not realize that it was *my life* they were discussing?

In the end, Judge Faulk did not lengthen my sentence. I shuffled out of the courtroom, past the horrified eyes of the people who knew me and was escorted back to the holding tank where I would wait for the other inmates to complete their hearings before we made the forty-five minute drive back to Ashfield.

Once we returned, I made a collect call to my parents. My mother was not home, which was probably best for both of us. I began to weep as I spoke to my dad, but I was not crying for any of the obvious reasons. I broke down as I shared with him the goodness of the Lord, and told him how much God had done for me. Even though I was calling from perhaps the most despicable place on earth, and had just learned that I would have to stay in prison for the remainder of my sentence, God had been good to me. My dad must have wondered how I could speak of God's goodness in the midst of such painful circumstances, but he did not question me. He could tell by my tears and by the conviction in my voice that with all of my heart, I *knew* God was good.

Chapter 21

Mission Accomplished

I was in a daze. Monday, April 18, 1994, had been long and grueling and strange. I had been awake since about 4:00 A.M., when two guards at Ashfield shattered my sleep by screaming, "Forsythe! Pack out!" as my cell door flung open. They escorted me down the long, dark corridor to the receiving and discharge area and handed me my civilian clothes.

As I dressed, I could hardly believe this part of my nightmare was finally over. I knew that Ashfield was like a black hole, a place inmates seemed to stay for long periods of time. One woman I met was still waiting to be transferred one-and-a-half years after her trial. The Lord had taken me into that hideous place there for a short season, and my assignment was completed. I was ready to leave.

The same two U.S. Marshals who had driven me from Benton to Ashfield ten days earlier arrived to transport me again. *Where will they take me this time?* I wondered. I learned the first time I was in transit not to ask.

"You must have some kind of attorney or know somebody pretty high up," one of the Marshals remarked. "We've never seen anybody get released from this place so fast." I had heard the stories. Indeed, I did know "somebody high up," if that was the language they wanted to use. It was the Lord who had orchestrated my quick release. It was He—not a prison warden, not a politician, not a government official—who was intervening, watching over me and ordering my steps with the precision of a watchmaker and the tenderness of a lamb. He was the one who would hold me through the uncertainty of the days and hours that lay ahead, even though the next moments would hurl shame at me in a way few other experiences could.

I never grew accustomed to the cruel click of handcuffs locking around my wrists or the harsh weight of shackles around my ankles. But there I was with those humiliating accessories again, preparing for yet another journey that would end in a place I would not know until I arrived. Only one thing was sure: my destination would be some sort of prison somewhere in the United States. I could not bear to think of all the possibilities.

I had prayed continually that I would be sent back to Benton. Throughout the re-sentencing and my time at Ashfield, I clung to the silent hope that I might somehow be totally released and sent home. But I had said repeatedly to the Lord, "If I have to go back to a prison, please let it be Benton." Still, I knew the government could have sent me absolutely anywhere.

I never thought I would actually be relieved to see the sign at the entrance to the federal prison at Benton. After my time at Ashfield, Benton did not look nearly as bad as it once did to me. At least it was familiar and at least I had friends there. It was certainly better than Ashfield, *much* better.

The Marshals stopped outside of the R and D building and a guard approached the police car. When she saw me, she was stunned and said, "Forsythe, what are you doing here? I don't have any paperwork on you." The Marshals informed her that they had received orders to transport me to Benton, to which she responded with a blank stare, as if she had no idea what they were talking about and did not really believe them. Again, she insisted that Benton had not received any paperwork pertaining to my transfer and mumbled something about how impossible it was for me to have gotten out of Ashfield.

The Marshals showed her their copy of the official transfer orders, and she had no choice but to process me in. I thought once again about Corrie ten Boom. She had not expected to be released from prison when she was, and when she wrote about that experience, she said: "His timing is perfect. His will is our hiding place."[5]

Yes. His timing was perfect. I had not been released to freedom, but His timing was perfect anyway. He had brought me back to Benton, which was the birthplace of my real relationship with Him and had become an unlikely hiding place in which He would teach me and train me and test me and conform me more and more into His image. He had answered my prayer to return, and given my options, this was certainly the best.

The check-in process this time was the same as it was when I first arrived at Benton. It included the dreaded strip search, which was less traumatic than it was the first time, but I did not ever escape that examination without fresh horror and a brand-new cloak of shame and degradation that rested upon me for a while afterwards. The only standard check-in procedure they allowed me to skip was the medical exam, which was a relief, and probably a small wonder because I looked so bad.

Before I proceeded to the room where I would be issued a uniform, an officer handed me the box that contained everything I had packed away ten days earlier. It was all there, and though I did not have much, I was relieved—even grateful—to see my possessions again. I chose a "new" uniform from a pile of rumpled clothes, picked out a pair of previously worn steel-toed work boots and socks—all the same items in all the same quantities I had been issued before. I never thought I would think a prison uniform was a step up from anything, but the clothes at Benton far surpassed the dirty orange jumpsuit and two left flip-flops I had worn at Ashfield.

Once I dressed in my uniform, gathered my box of belongings and all of the paperwork had been completed, the officer assigned me to a cell and a guard escorted me to it. To my total amazement, they assigned me to the same cell where I had lived before! In fact, I even ended up in my old familiar bottom bunk. There seemed to be an unofficial code of seniority that relegated top bunks to the newest inmates and awarded bottom bunks to those who had been there longer. I *really* did not want to start at the top again. I managed to smile inside as I thought about how much the Lord cared for the details, how aware He was of the seemingly small things that made a big difference to me.

When the guard left, I stood in the cell, amazed by the turn of events that had brought me back so quickly. I did not know how it happened; I just knew that the Lord had done a paperwork miracle.

Someone was watching as I returned to the dormitory— my friend, Liz. She had been shocked the day she heard that I was gone. I had not had a chance to say goodbye to anyone or to tell her that I was leaving, so she had no idea what had happened. She was not convinced I was gone until she went to my cell that day and saw with her own eyes that my bunk was bare and my locker was empty. Though baffled by my sudden exit, she desperately hoped I had been released and knew that she would hear from me as soon as possible. Until then, she determined to pray.

Then one day, the prison was abuzz with gossip that some new inmates were expected, and somehow Liz heard a rumor that I might be returning with that group. She was perched on her bunk, from which she could see everyone who entered the dorm—and she was looking for me.

I did not have many journal entries from those days, perhaps because I was so weak and so exhausted. Liz, however, remembered it well.

> *They say it's so humiliating—that Ashfield. Mary came back looking very weak, but her spirits were good. She was pale; she was puny. She looked very, very bad. But whatever battle she went to fight, she won. I had no idea what she had been through, but she came back with her peace of mind. It was astounding. She was so desperate for more of God and so broken—weak in her body, but powerful, so powerful, in spirit.*
>
> *Something happened to her there because she was so different when she came back—more broken. Everything about her was different, dramatically different. It was like she went to the pit of the enemy's camp and took something back. She came back with more power. She was confident in God when she left, but she was bold, so bold, when she got back.*

I was not aware of some of the changes Liz observed, but I must have realized at least some of the incredible brokenness that occurred in me at Ashfield because of my first journal entry after my return:

4/20/94: Read Prison Letters *by Corrie ten Boom. She says that God never gives us any burden to break our backs, but only to bow our knees.*

I could never remember a more difficult burden than my experience at Ashfield, but the Lord had used it to humble me and, in the process, to make me stronger, bolder, more dependent on Him than ever.

Something life changing happened during my ten days at Ashfield. I saw and heard and smelled unspeakably horrible things and endured inexpressible hardship. Thankful for triumph over those days of despair, I was glad to be back at Benton and eager to regain my daily rhythm. Re-entering life at Benton was more difficult than I thought it would be, and after being back for several days, I revealed my struggle in my journal:

4/24/94: The enemy of my soul has tried to get me to focus on what I do <u>not</u> have. Quickly I must remember what I do have. Jesus has awakened me from the dead. I have a huge opportunity to exercise my faith. I have chosen to believe Psalm 91:15, "I will deliver [you] and honor [you]." I have chosen to believe Deuteronomy 28:6, 7, "You will be blessed when you come in and blessed when you go out . . .the enemies who rise up against you . . . will come at you from one direction but flee from you in seven" (NIV).

I think of how God got me out of Ashfield in only ten days. My papers were not even at Benton upon my return. Before I left Ashfield, Rita said, "Your work here is finished." I truly believe I will not be in prison one day more than God deems.

The Holy Spirit also showed me a scripture to help me understand my experience at Ashfield, and to assure me again that my times were in His hands. A chill coursed through me when I read the ancient words of Revelation 2:10, words that reached through thousands of years and yet could not have been more poignant or more relevant to me at that moment: "Do not fear any of those things which you are about to suffer. Indeed, the devil is about to throw some of you into prison, that you may be tested, and you will have tribulation ten days. Be faithful unto death, and I will give you the crown of life."

I was in awe as I read those words, which seemed like a modern-day chronicle of my ten days at Ashfield. I marveled at the way the Lord spoke to me through that verse and put my maximum-security experience into a perspective I could not have gained on my own.

One morning not long after my return, I was shocked to see my name on the daily call-out sheet and to read that I had been ordered to report to the office of Mr. Taylor, the associate warden, later that day.

As I looked again at my name on the call-out sheet, I wondered, *What could* this *possibly mean?* I had no idea why Mr. Taylor would want to see me. I had never been ordered to the administrative offices before but had known women who had gone to meetings there and never returned! It was a perfect opportunity for my imagination to run wild, but I could not allow myself to even consider the numerous possibilities ahead of me. I had a choice: I could be anxious, or I could trust the Lord. I decided to trust. He had so obviously ordered my steps in the past that I knew I could count on Him this time too.

Physically, going to see Mr. Taylor was easy. I just had to show up at his office on time, sign in and wait for his assistant to call my number. But internally, it was not so simple. There was such conflict inside of me—an incredible battle between fearful uncertainty and the unshakable conviction that the Lord was there for me. I had to keep reminding myself that He—and only He—was in charge of the consequences of this meeting.

Chapter 22

Flying Lessons

The Lord did indeed have a new challenge for me. He had a plan, and Mr. Taylor had good news. Of all the 800-something inmates, twenty-four had been hand-picked for two different work assignments outside the prison. He informed me that I had been chosen, along with ten or twelve others, to work in an office at a nearby mental health clinic: Mental Health and Mental Retardation Authority of Benton Valley, which we abbreviated, "MHMR." Being selected for this assignment was a great honor, one that evoked the jealousy of many other inmates.

When Mr. Taylor said to me, "You will report for work at 7:30 next Monday morning," I responded, "Mr. Taylor, I really appreciate being considered for this program. I'll pray about it and get back to you. When do you need to know?" He quickly informed me that a refusal to accept this assignment would send me to solitary confinement and could mean a transfer to another prison. He told me that even a mother eagle pushes her babies out of the nest when the time is right for them to learn to fly. When I heard that, I knew the Holy

Spirit was giving me a message, telling me that it was time for me to spread my wings and begin to learn to fly again.

I had completed more than half of my time at Benton and knew that the day would come when I would finally be released from prison. When it did, I would need to get a job, find a place to live and interact on many levels with people who were not either inmates or prison employees. Working at MHMR would be an opportunity to re-enter society gradually, and the Lord was orchestrating circumstances in my life while I was still in prison to make moving back into the free world easier when I got out. Taking the job at MHMR would also mean being able to leave the prison grounds five days a week and being able to wear my few civilian clothes instead of a prison uniform to work every day. It would mean a tiny taste of freedom Monday through Friday, but it would also mean having to endure the check-in process every single day, the possibility of frequent strip searches and random urinalyses.

I could hardly bear the thought of leaving the prison compound every day, living several hours almost like a free woman and then having to go back. There were many volunteers at MHMR, and only certain staff members knew which ones were from Benton, so for the first time in almost two years I would be around people who did not know I was a prisoner. Even though I would not be identified by a uniform or a nametag, I still had the invisible label of "convict" stitched on the inside of me. I was frightened by the idea of stepping into an environment where I felt so different from, and so inferior to, everyone else.

At Benton I had intentionally done everything I could think of to keep from becoming institutionalized. I put my napkin in my lap during meals; thanked the women who served me in the chow hall; said "please" and "excuse me," "ma'am" and "sir"; and remembered the manners and simple courtesies my parents had taught me. I also made a conscious decision not to allow the common prison slang to become part of my vocabulary. Nevertheless, a person can only do so much to avoid being institutionalized when she lives in an institution.

I knew I would struggle to adapt to the new work environment and to being around people whose daily realities were so totally different from mine, people who could never truly understand my life. At least in prison all things were relatively equal. Being a criminal is a little less awkward when everyone around you is one too. I could hardly believe the strange sense of comfort I had developed about my familiar living conditions. And I could hardly believe how hesitant I was to make this first move toward eventual release.

But I knew the Holy Spirit had spoken and that He was leading me to the next step on my path to freedom. The time had come for me to venture beyond bars, even with my misgivings about the transition. The Holy Spirit had opened a door of opportunity for me, and I needed to walk through it—even though I was scared, even though I was reluctant and even though I was ashamed.

One of the good things about working at MHMR was that my friend Charlotte had also been chosen for the program there. Charlotte was a Remnant Group sister, several years my senior, a mother figure to many of the women at Benton, and someone I had come to appreciate early in my stay. I was glad to know our new job assignments would allow us to spend more time together.

The morning of our first day at MHMR, I dressed in one of my two personal outfits, glad I did not have to wear a uniform, and went to the chow hall to pick up the white cardboard lunchbox issued to inmates who worked off-site.

With my lunchbox (which contained four pieces of white bread, two slices of cheese, a portion of meat and, hopefully, a piece of fruit), I boarded the prison van with the other inmates and took an apprehensive ride to the mental health clinic, knowing that it was clearly time to stand on the edge of the nest and flap my wings.

I was assigned to help the director of the children's department, Lisa Saunders, and one of my duties was to answer the telephone. Most people would not consider that a particular challenge, but it threw me into a panic. Before I began my job assignment at MHMR, I had not spoken on the phone to anyone besides my family and Mike. My calls from Benton were limited to ten minutes each, they had to be collect and my conversations could be recorded at random. Just knowing that there were no restrictions on my phone use was a giant leap toward freedom for me.

The first time the office telephone rang, I could do nothing but stare at the receiver, paralyzed by fear. With my hand shaking, I finally picked it up, and with my voice trembling, I finally answered, "MHMR children's department." I could tell from that one experience that this part of my transition out of prison life was going to be much more challenging and more involved than I had anticipated. Gradually, I became comfortable answering the phone and performing other duties I was assigned, and after several weeks, my supervisor recognized my office skills and allowed me to use them by increasing my responsibilities.

The job was good for me. One of my co-workers in the children's department was a warm and wonderful Christian lady named Fran. Charlotte and I often ate lunch with her and soon realized that our common faith and love for the Lord tore down the barrier that sometimes existed between

employees and prison volunteers. This God-ordained friendship, combined with the practical experience I was gaining
at MHMR, made my new work assignment an important
piece of preparation for my eventual release. Not long after I
started working there I remembered how reluctant I was to
take this step and wrote in my journal:

> *11/8/94: MHMR is good. I fought it at first, not know-
> ing if it was the enemy or the Lord. I forgot that nothing
> touches me that hasn't passed through Him first.*

Indeed, He had allowed the opportunity at MHMR in my
life and it had "passed through Him first." Although the working environment was pleasant, the rules for inmates were strict.
I remember one rule well: we were only permitted to eat what
was in our lunch boxes and any food we purchased at the commissary and took with us. If there happened to be a party, or any
occasion for which an employee brought food to the office, we
were forbidden to eat it. If one inmate broke even one rule, we
could all be punished and the consequences would be severe.

Our lunchboxes were important because they contained
the only food we could eat while we were working, but mine
became especially important because the Holy Spirit used it
to teach me a lesson. It was amazing what a little something
different could do when people were locked in a place where
everything was so terribly *the same.* That was the case with
my lunchbox.

The serious sin of pride came back to me packed in those
silly lunchboxes more than once. They tempted me to gloat
for two reasons. First, unlike so many things in prison, few
inmates carried them. I had something that everyone else
did not. Second, no one could see through them. My entire
existence in prison felt like a gigantic windowpane. Nothing,

absolutely nothing, was private. Everyone could see or hear everything except my thoughts, so my boxed lunches were the most personal thing I had, just a small piece of privacy in a package.

The fact that my lunches were not readily visible inspired the curiosity and envy of the general prison population. Every morning, I left for work carrying my little secret-in-a-box, well aware that other inmates noticed. I was tempted to think that my non-see-through lunchbox and my off-site work assignment made me better than everyone else. I almost fell back into the old familiar thought pattern of superiority, but once I recognized that my lunchbox could be a source of pride, and therefore a source of sin, I began to resist the temptation. And one day, the Holy Spirit gave me an idea that turned my lunchbox into a blessing instead of a curse.

A little boy named Nathan regularly visited MHMR. He had been severely abused—neglected to the point that he could not hear because pebbles had been jammed into his ear canals for years and, therefore, his speech was terribly underdeveloped. His grandmother was nearly destitute but faithfully brought him to counseling each week. We tried to communicate with him as best we could, and sometimes he understood and sometimes it seemed that he did not. But there was one time we were certain he knew exactly what we had in mind.

Christmas was coming. Charlotte and I remarked that it would be nice for Nathan's grandmother to have a present, but we certainly could not go out shopping for a gift! Then I had an idea. "Charlotte, let's put our meat and our cheese in the freezer every day and save it for Nathan's grandmother!" She was delighted and eagerly agreed. Both of us realized that, although we had nothing material to offer, we did receive a lunchbox every morning and that it provided us with something to give. Our hearts were warmed by the thought that we could do something for someone else at Christmas time. So there we were—two prisoners, in conspiracy to bless someone!

We started stockpiling meat and cheese around Thanksgiving. During the holiday weekend, I pondered the things for which I could be thankful. My journal entry from November 24, 1994, best captured the way I felt that day:

11/24/94: Thanksgiving. There must be some mistake. I am still in prison. Circumstances are seemingly unchanged, yet—Oh, Father, the joy. Pure, true heart joy. I have been so blessed by His presence lately. During prayer time—oh, how indescribable. Fullness of joy is truly in His presence. Victory has come.

So many priceless lessons and incredible moments with Him. His love filling me so that there is peace—such peace and assurance that He knows, He cares and He loves. I look back and see how He has taught me to praise, pray, worship and fellowship…

After Thanksgiving, we inmates returned to our jobs at MHMR. Through the end of November and into December, Charlotte and I continued to save our food for Nathan's grandmother. During his last visit before Christmas, we asked Nathan, "Wouldn't you like to give your grandmother a present?" His eyes began to sparkle and an enormous grin came to his face. We packed the meat and cheese we had been storing and handed it to him with a pleasure that nothing and no one could take from us. Even though we lived in prison, a place designed to steal our joy and stifle our generosity, we had been able to give Nathan the joy of giving—and that was the Lord's Christmas gift to me.

Chapter 23

Comfort and Joy

The 1994 holiday season was challenging, as I found my-self not only faced with the completion of another calendar year, but with a variety of other endings. Two days before Christmas, my friend and cellmate, Lottie, was released. I sat on my bunk and watched, saying little, as she gathered her few belongings, emptied her locker and removed the sheets from her bed.

The Lord had given me a true treasure in Lottie. This young, quiet, Spanish woman had been my cellmate since her first day at Benton—ten or eleven months earlier—and had quickly become a friend and a regular part of the Remnant Group. Soon after her arrival, we discovered that we were on the same journey, two pilgrim prisoners walking together, longing for more of Jesus.

For Lottie, incarceration meant leaving at home a hus-band and young children she loved with all her heart. It meant being unable to cook their meals and wash their clothes, to kiss them goodbye as they left home in the mornings, to make a birthday cake or attend a school play. But the weight of that burden did not crush her. Instead, it pressed out of her a passion for the Lord and brought forth deep and rapid growth in Him.

As I thought of Lottie's earthly family, I realized that she and I were family too. We had the same Father and were sisters in the Lord. I had already learned that the Lord chose my friends and was in control of their comings and goings in my life. I knew, as Lottie was leaving prison to walk into the free world, that the Lord was asking me once again to walk more closely with Him. After she was gone, I wrote about her departure on the pages of my journal:

> *12/23/94: It has been a joyful morning, for the hand of the Lord opened the gate and my cellmate (Lottie) left this morning. No words could express my thankfulness to my Father for such a precious gift. We had communion this morning together and shared a tearful prayer. I look back and I can only give thanks, for my life has been so blessed with her friendship. As iron sharpens iron, so does one man sharpen another.*
>
> *I think of Jesus and how lonely He must have been. The friends He'd spent more than 3 years with—praying, teaching and living—left Him. Not only did they leave Him, but they denied Him. Yes, a friend has left me, but Jesus understands.*

Yes. Jesus understood. He also understood the pain in my heart as I struggled to accept what was becoming clear—that Mike and I were growing apart and that our relationship was quickly fizzling. Having to embrace that truth was doubly difficult because not only was I losing the man I loved, I was living in a place where loneliness was larger than life. I had found loneliness to be one of the most poignant perils of prison, a danger that threatened to break apart a person's heart, one solitary moment at a time. Even in the presence of other inmates, people felt totally isolated. I knew, because I had struggled so much with the heartache of being away from Mike.

The longer we were separated by prison walls, the longer our lives progressed down parallel tracks that rarely crossed. We were not only apart from each other physically, we had grown apart spiritually as well. I could sense the promptings of the Holy Spirit, nudging me to release him. I prayed; I fasted; and I sought answers in the Word. The scripture that jumped off the page repeatedly was Ecclesiastes 11:1, "Cast your bread upon the waters...."

I felt the Holy Spirit saying that I *had* to cast my bread upon the waters, to totally surrender my relationship with Mike, and that if it really was "mine," the relationship would be restored. The next time he came to visit, my wrenching decision had been made. I said, "Mike, it's okay for you to see other people." We both knew our relationship was ending, but we both cried.

Now, I was alone. My heart hurt so deeply I would not have been surprised had it given up and quit beating. Mike was gone—gone back to a life of freedom while I remained behind bars. But in my remaining, I discovered the Lord in ways I had not known Him before. He gave me the grace to go on without allowing my emotions to control and consume me. He taught me that He was Lord of emotions and Lord of lonely days, Lord of relationships, Lord of every detail of my life. I reminded myself that nothing could touch me that did not pass through the filter of His love.

I faced another tremendous challenge immediately— Christmas in prison, my second one at Benton. (The previous Christmas had been so unspeakably devastating that I was not even able to write about it. My journal page was empty on that day.)

Every Christmas Day during 4:00 P.M. count, all of the inmates had to stand beside our bunks while guards walked from cell to cell mumbling, "Merry Christmas" as they handed each inmate a "present"—a brown paper bag that usually contained several pieces of candy, a few laundry tokens and perhaps a comb or some other small personal item. As the guard handed me my gift, I said, "Thank you. Merry Christmas to you." I had not wanted to say anything, but I knew that was the right thing to do.

I despised the prison holiday ritual. It was degrading—undoubtedly the most piercing reminder of the fact that I was a criminal, an outcast, a prisoner. The whole occasion would have been easier to endure if no one had acknowledged Christmas at all. I did receive cards from friends and family, but gifts were prohibited. I did not need shiny packages or bows, however. I needed the Lord. I needed His presence so much more than I needed presents from other people. He was all I wanted; He was all I had; and He was enough. Everything else was a lesser allegiance.

There was no tinsel to be found at Benton, no trees or ornaments or sparkling decorations, no home-baked goodies, no twinkling lights. But I did not need any of that. I had enjoyed Christmases past filled with presents and parties, but void of God. This year, I had so little—all of my material gifts in a brown paper sack. But my heart was full and on December 25, 1994, I recorded my Christmas reflections:

12/25/94: Praise God in all things, and I thank Him for another Christmas with no distractions. I had a peaceful five-mile walk this morning. I just sought Him so hard.

And I know submission is the doorway to peace. I think about the condition of my heart this time last year and how He has matured me. For this year, I desire to live less for myself and more for others and for Him. He is Master. He is the Potter. He is the Great Shepherd. He is God.

The day after Christmas, I endured another one of prison's dishonorable rituals—a "shake down"—guards barging into my cell and searching my locker. I thought a shake down on the day after Christmas was particularly cruel, but I found a remarkable inner peace during that process, a peace that could only have come from heaven:

12/26/94: Even though guards came into my cell and shook down my locker, there was peace in my heart. This was a Christmas gift from my Father. I can only look ahead.

Having the guards come in and shake down my locker was always unnerving. I marveled at the peace within my heart as they tore open my locker door and rummaged through everything I had. They conducted these intrusions at random, searching for anything illegal. We were allowed to have ten photographs, which we affixed to the inside of our locker doors with institutional toothpaste, and the guards could confiscate all of an inmate's pictures if she had too many.

The entire process was totally dehumanizing. Although I always kept my locker neat and had nothing to hide, having the guards thoroughly inspect my few possessions was a fresh reminder of the fact that I had no privacy and no respect. The tiny space I had did not even belong to me, but was readily accessible to any guard taken by a whim to see what was in it. And, I could not forget one "close call" that happened with my locker.

One reason I despised shakedowns so much was that my locker had once been the target of a set-up, a scheme that, if successful, could have resulted in up to five additional years in prison for me. One afternoon, I returned to my cell after my job at MHMR to a surprise. At that time, I only had one cellmate and she had been transferred while I was at work that day because she was caught stealing food from the kitchen. When I returned to see that she had moved out, I thought, *Ahh! An empty cell! A whole night all by myself!* and I was overcome with gratitude as I relished this rare, unexpected gift of time alone.

"Oh, yes! Thank You, Lord!" I said softly.

But the Holy Spirit said something else: "Danger. Danger."

I continued my celebration. "This is great! No one will be snoring tonight. No one will be getting up and down to go to the bathroom. No one will be tossing or turning or shaking the bunks. I'll have the entire cell all to myself all night long!"

But I kept hearing the Holy Spirit warn me: "Danger. Danger." I ignored this divine alert, slightly irritated that He did not join my delight, and began to wonder if it was *His* voice I was hearing, or the voice of the enemy, trying to steal the pleasure of my night alone.

I glanced around my cell, concluded that everything was fine and resumed my thoughts of the privacy and calm that would accompany my night of solitude. "Thank You, Lord, for making this possible."

But the message would not stop. No matter how hard I tried, I could not drown out that one repeated word, "Danger. Danger." And then I heard a clear instruction: "Look behind your locker."

Behind my locker! *For what?* I wondered. *Besides, I can't look behind my locker. That's against the rules!* Moving a locker even a tiny bit was prohibited, because if we scratched the floor while doing so, we would be punished. But the Holy Spirit was relentless.

Finally, I scooted my locker away from the wall far enough to peek behind it and was horrified by what I saw. Someone had secured a small stash of drugs, put them in a clear plastic bag and taken great pains to stick the bag to the back of my locker. What a perfect trap for a former pharmacist! I shuddered when I dared to think of what would have happened had the guards discovered those pills. I ripped them off my locker, hid them in my pocket, carefully slid my locker back against the wall, took the drugs to the bathroom and flushed them down the nearest toilet.

The Holy Spirit saved me once again. There was gentleness in His urgency as He sounded the alarm for me and prompted me to move my locker—which seemed crazy to me. But He knew. He knew exactly what the enemy had done: found someone to execute an evil plot against me. And the Holy Spirit demolished the devil's design with a steady signal that, once I heeded, kept me from potentially having to spend more time behind bars. Remembering that experience, I marveled again at the supernatural gift of peace the Holy Spirit had given me that December day during the shakedown. Incredible peace deep inside of me, ruling over my turbulent circumstances.

Tension and anxiety and fear seemed to bounce off the very walls of the prison, and the atmosphere was pure chaos. A person could never find peace in an environment like that if she searched for it anywhere but deep inside her own heart. No one and nothing could bring peace except Jesus. I stood in awe of another mighty act of quiet grace as I thought about how I endured the shake down completely unruffled.

Another miracle I recognized that day was that, as I had written in my journal, "I can only look ahead." It was true. I could only look ahead—and because of what the Holy Spirit had done in my heart, I could look ahead without fear. I could not and would not look behind me. I could only fix my gaze on Jesus and believe that He had a plan for my life beyond the confines of a federal prison. Even though I had no earthly reason to have hope for my future, the Holy Spirit was still whispering destiny to me. He had begun to put dreams in my heart and to even speak to others about His plans for me. I continued my journal entry on the day after Christmas, remembering that He had shown Lottie, before she left, a part of His heart for me:

> *12/26/94: I thought about the vision Lottie shared with me right before she left. The Lord showed her a map with Brazil, Africa and other countries on it. She was praying for me. Then she saw a folder with my passport in it. The folder said, "Restitution is paid and passport is in order."*
>
> *All of this made me think about how we must die daily—carrying the cross every day. I want His plan and His highest.*

The Holy Spirit brought two scriptures to my mind that afternoon, reminding me again that indeed, we *must* die daily. I read Luke 9:23, which says, "If anyone desires to come after Me, let him deny himself, and take up his cross daily, and follow Me." I also read John 12:24, which says, "Most assuredly, I say to you, unless a grain of wheat falls into the ground and dies, it remains alone; but if it dies, it produces much grain."

The Spirit was teaching me that His life could only increase in me as my own life decreased. I knew enough to know that I certainly had not done a good job trying to be in control of my life. (Look where I ended up!) But I also knew that the Holy Spirit was longing to heal and restore and perfectly clean up the mess I had made of myself. Dying daily—loving by choice, preferring others over myself, and putting thoughts and fleshly tendencies under the rule of the Word—was not easy, but it was worth it.

The holiday season continued, as did the Spirit's dealings with me in the areas of trust and peace. Christmas had passed, but I still had to endure New Year's Day. How desperately I wanted to be free! How I longed to think about the new year with thoughts that it might bring my release! But I knew that, without a miracle, it would not be.

The Holy Spirit knew. He knew my longings and my every thought. He walked me gently through those days and spoke to me about the Lord's timing—another opportunity for greater peace and trust to take deeper root in my heart:

12/28/94: How truly He is the Master. For it must be in His timing. The holidays are so tough! But the Holy Spirit has been speaking to me about the timing of the Lord. His timing is part of His will. What if the fruit developed too soon on a tree? The trunk would not be strong enough nor the roots deep enough to hold the fruit. The tree and the fruit would both collapse. But the Father knows just when to command the fruit to grow. God is in control. All is under His loving control!

He is showing me how to reach out. The first miracle is in my heart and in my attitude. It is not just reaching out to those I want to reach out to, for that is still my plan. How easy it is to love those who love us! Oh Lord, let me learn quickly. Let my heart be opened totally to You!

While MHMR was closed for the holidays, prison officials regarded those of us who worked there as "unassigned," which meant to them that we were available for any duty they wanted to give us—and I always had to pick up cigarette butts. Needless to say, I was relieved to be back in my routine when I went back to work on December 29:

12/29/94: Back to MHMR. It was strange today because inmates from the county jail came to get treated. They were in the dirty orange jumpsuits and shackled. I knew we were the same (inmates), but I did not have on shackles.

I heard one of the guards say that he had gone into law enforcement because a policeman had saved his life. Just as this guard followed the man who saved him, once we see how Jesus saved us, we will follow Him.

I had seen how Jesus had saved me—not just reserving a place for me in heaven, but *really* saving me, really changing me and continuing to work in my heart in ways that astounded me. I no longer followed Him out of a childhood sense of fear or obligation, but out of a grown-up passion for the One who saved me in a grand and glorious way. I had fallen in love with Him to the point that I followed Him eagerly. As much as I hoped to somehow be released from prison in the new year, there was really only one place I truly wanted to be, and that was right next to Him, safely walking to the beat of His perfect timing.

Chapter 24

Learning to Love

They called me "that woman who prays." As word spread that I prayed for people, women began to tell me their needs, struggles and disappointments and to ask for prayer. But until I learned better, I asked those who came for help to come back later because I had to finish my Bible reading.

In my immaturity, I thought I was being spiritual to devote myself to prayer and Bible study at the expense of extending love to other people, but I later learned that I was actually being proud and selfish! Slowly, the Spirit began to show me how deceived I was and taught me how important it was to take time to talk with other people even at what I might consider inconvenient moments.

At first, I stopped asking them to come back later, but did not close my Bible when they entered my cell—a sign that I really did not want to be bothered. Then, I began to close my Bible, but did not ask them to sit down. After going through several increments of hospitality, I finally came to the point where I understood what the Spirit was trying to teach me. He wanted me to welcome an inmate and focus on her situation and need. The process of pruning me away from my selfish tendencies had taken some time, and I was glad when I thought it was over!

But it was not over and it was a more complex process than I realized. So many layers of selfishness needed to be peeled off so many areas of my life. I finally came to understand that every time I thought I had mastered a specific lesson, I had not mastered it at all, but had simply gained enough proficiency to be taken to a deeper level. Just as principles of higher mathematics are based on simple arithmetic, aspects of spiritual maturity are rooted in basic, foundational principles and disciplines. One of the foundational elements of love is sacrifice—the polar opposite of selfishness. And as I began a new year, I found myself attacked again by a familiar enemy—me!

I felt that I had come so far from the greedy, self-centered woman I was when I first went to prison, but I was more selfish than I knew. I had learned to give my time and energy to people who needed a listening ear or a prayer or an encouraging word. I thought I had learned to give, to share things when it cost me and to live sacrificially. But when the Holy Spirit asked me to give away one of my favorite, most precious possessions, I saw for myself that there still lived in me a desire to cling to what was mine.

One morning as I was putting on my lipstick, the Holy Spirit spoke to me and said, "Mary, give that away today." And I engaged in a discussion with Him that went something like this.

"I hardly have anything left! I brought this lipstick in from outside, and I mean, this is *nice, expensive* lipstick. It's my one tiny luxury! If I give this away, I can't get any more like it for, maybe, *years!*"

I could tell my protest was not working, but continued anyway.

"I just don't have anything anymore. It's like I have nothing, and You're asking me to give away the nothing I've got!"

Still, I could hear the Holy Spirit saying, "Mary, give it away today," and finally, I relented. Later that day, I saw an inmate and knew instantly that she was the one to whom I was to give the lipstick. So I gave it and remembered the day someone had left everything I needed from the commissary on my bunk when I had no money. Perhaps that inmate, in some way, needed lipstick. Maybe she did; maybe she didn't, but I believed that, somehow, it carried a message from the Lord to her. I never knew for certain what the lipstick meant, but found the joy of obedience and sacrifice in giving it away. From that moment on, I began to see "my" possessions, time, money and energy as commodities that did not really belong to me anyway, but like the lipstick, were often given to me so that I could turn around and use them to help someone else.

How much the Holy Spirit had changed me! The incident with my lipstick caused me to reflect on my life: being driven to make money so that I could fill my life with possessions I deemed impressive; buying myself the most fashionable clothes, the finest wines and expensive cosmetics (like lipstick!). And I remembered reviewing my investments and checking my bank accounts to see just how much I had accumulated. I had despised myself, but I had also been determined to give myself as much as I possibly could. I enjoyed giving to other people, but not when the gifts required any measure of sacrifice on my part. Always selfish; never satisfied.

But that began to change after I met the Holy Spirit and began to surrender my life to Him. Until that point, I alone had worn the crown over my life. I had coronated myself and subjected every aspect of my existence to whatever I wanted. But following Jesus required submitting to new rulership. I had to step down from the throne of my life, hand over my scepter and allow the Lord absolute dominion, complete control of everything about me.

As selfishness attempted a fresh assault on my soul, I remembered again Corrie ten Boom, who had inspired me since I first read her book entitled *The Hiding Place*. She called selfishness a cancer and wrote about her own struggle with it when she was forced to stand outside in the biting German winter during roll call at Ravensbruck:

> *And as the cold increased, so did the special temptation of concentration-camp life: the temptation to think only of oneself. It took a thousand cunning forms. I quickly discovered that when I maneuvered our way toward the middle of the roll call formation we had a little protection from the wind. I knew this was self-centered ... How easy it was to give it other names! ... Selfishness had a life of its own ... and even if it wasn't right—it wasn't so very wrong, was it? ... Oh, this was the great ploy of Satan in that kingdom of his: to display such blatant evil that one could almost believe one's secret sins didn't matter.*[6]

I agreed. No matter what happened in my surroundings, no matter how perverse or mean-spirited or hard-hearted the people around me were, I could not allow myself to fail in love. I could not harbor any "secret sins." Though no sins are secrets to God, some sins exist only behind the heart's closed doors, hidden from other people. In prison, selfishness was an easy secret sin. Most people there were selfish, so no one really noticed when the "me-first monster" reared its ugly head.

Selfishness is silently but brutally opposed to love; and God *is* love. To be selfish is to violate His law of love. If I were going to follow Him, I simply could not allow selfishness even the smallest space to breathe in my heart. I found repeatedly that I had to purposefully discipline my thoughts and actions so as to extricate that greedy disease.

> *1/6/95: I think of* The Hiding Place. *How true it is. The cancer can so easily mutate—spread and grow so fast. The cancer of "self." First I found myself sitting at the front of the van so I could get checked in and out first. Not considering others. Oh, how sneaky the enemy is and how easily he creeps in.*

I had done something that reminded me of Corrie's maneuvering to get herself and Betsie into the middle of the roll call formation so that other people would block some of the wind from them. I had not done that, of course, but I had jockeyed for a position in the van that transported us from MHMR to Benton. Every day, when we returned from work, we went through a check-in process during which the guards questioned us, patted us down and conducted strip searches at random. I had figured out that people who sat in the back of the van and were the last ones off tended to get strip searched, while those who got off first usually escaped that traumatic experience.

I always made my way quickly to the van as soon as the workday was over so that I could secure a seat close to the front. No one wanted to be strip searched, and I was glad to have discovered how to keep myself from having to endure it most of the time. One afternoon, I hurried to the van, as usual, after work and headed for my favorite seat near the front. Suddenly, the Holy Spirit spoke to me and told me to wait and let everyone else board the van first. I was almost overwhelmed by His request, not because He was asking me to extend the courtesy of allowing others to get on ahead of me, but because I knew exactly what the potential consequences of waiting would be—a strip search.

In the past, I had successfully protected myself against that wretched appraisal, but that day, the Holy Spirit was asking me not to consider myself, but to prefer others and to willingly subject myself to the most demeaning aspect of the check-in process. After all the other inmates were settled in the van, the only seat left was on the very back row. I climbed on and slid into that seat, hating the thought of what probably awaited me when we returned to Benton, but hoping against the odds.

Standing in line anxiously waiting to see if my name would be called, I heard Mrs. Wilson bark, "Forsythe! Over here!" as she ordered me into the strip search room. I knew what was coming. I had survived it time after time. Knowing what it would be like and anticipating its horror pushed me almost to the edge of my sanity. *I cannot go through this one more time,* I thought, and I especially dreaded having to be searched by Mrs. Wilson, who was probably the harshest, rudest inspector of all. I was afraid I might break down under the pressure—that I might snap mentally or emotionally.

In that moment of excruciating despair, I suddenly had a vision. I saw Jesus, in His most humiliating state, hanging on the cross. It was as though He could see all the way through time to me, standing there so desperately, teetering on the razor thin edge of an emotional cliff. The vision captured my full attention, and I heard Him say, "Mary, I understand."

Those simple words had so much strength, so much ability to hold me and carry me through what was about to happen. A supernatural peace washed over me and lifted me above everything about that particular strip search. I endured it as though it were happening to someone else, and it failed to impact me that time the way it had so many times before.

One week later, the Holy Spirit was still revealing the selfish condition of my heart and prodding me toward victory, but it was not a battle easily won.

1/13/95: The enemy would have us concentrate on things we don't have, people and places we are removed from. God wants us to know what we do have in Jesus. I read Ephesians 1:15-21.

The Spirit was taking me through rigorous inner training, calling me yet again away from relying on anything—anything—that existed in me, in my own intellect or in my own strength. I jotted a note in my journal almost as an afterthought. It was undated, but recorded in early 1995, and seemed to summarize what the Spirit was asking of me. It was short but clear, and it did not require explanation or elaboration:

To honor God, give Him authority over your thinking and give Him your body as a living sacrifice.

The Holy Spirit was dealing deeply with some of my invisible issues—my motives, my intentions—and loosening my heart's grip on myself, leading me to new places of loving Him and loving others. I struggled. The first three weeks of the new year had been intense, and at the end of the third week, I journaled:

1/21/95: I know the Lord puts no more on us than we can bear. Sometimes I wish I wasn't built to bear so much! But truly these are light afflictions.

As difficult as prison life was, the Holy Spirit never left

me without encouragement. At times it might have seemed minor, but nothing was minor when it came from His hand. He gave me an extra-special dose of encouragement soon after my journey through the sinful land of selfishness:

> *1/27/95: How sweet the Lord is! Charlotte and I prayed in the prayer closet at the chapel today. I needed encouragement! I shared my testimony with her. As I told her about my past and how I used to travel so much, it was as if it struck a chord in her. Charlotte said, "I just got a picture that the experience of going into foreign countries will be used in future work for the Lord." He knew I needed to hear that. We sang songs of praise and lifted holy hands to the Father.*

I felt as though Corrie ten Boom had been my cellmate for the entire month of January. In certain ways, we had experienced so many of the same things. In other ways, we could not have been more different, but as I had done often, I recalled her words in my journal as a personal message of encouragement and hope:

> *1/27/95: I remember something Corrie ten Boom wrote: When Jesus is with you the worst can happen but the best remains.*

Once again, she was right. I could not remember where I read it, but I drew strength from this nugget of truth purchased by Corrie's personal suffering, a truth she paid for with her life experience. I was beginning to understand what she meant. I had spent years of my life far from Jesus, only to discover that nothing good accompanies a life without His presence. At Benton, the worst had happened to me in so many ways, but Jesus was with me. And there, nothing but the best remained.

As the weeks progressed, Corrie ten Boom continued to influence me through stories of her life, and the Spirit continued to call me to fresh surrender and obedience. One of the women who worked at MHMR had been asking questions about the Lord, and I wanted to give her a Bible. Because I could not hop in my car and drive to a bookstore, I knew that I had to obtain a Bible inside the prison and take it out to her. One more time, I remembered my "friend" from *The Hiding Place*.

Corrie and her sister, Betsie, treasured the Scriptures and miraculously smuggled a small copy of the Word into the concentration camp where they were imprisoned. Trying to hide that little Book of Life under her thin cotton dress, Corrie knew that it bulged enough to be noticed by anyone who looked in her direction, but the guards never saw it, and she made it into Ravensbruck death camp with the living Word no one could kill. Where they needed to get a Bible from the outside into their prison, I needed to get one from the inside out.

2/14/95: I smuggled a Bible out to Alice at MHMR yesterday. Corrie's story helped me to know how to pray. I know angels were on guard all around me.

Amazing. As much as I had struggled with selfishness, over time the Holy Spirit worked love into my heart to the point that I was willing to risk severe disciplinary action just to get God's Word into the hands of a desperate woman. Only He could have given me the courage to love like that.

As He continued to teach me to love others, He also revealed His love for me, which caused me to love Him more and more. It was a wonderful cycle, this flow of love from Him to me, from me to Him and to others, and then from Him to me in glorious, constant repetition.

2/20/95: I am just in awe. I have seen the Holy Spirit's ministry so clearly and in so many ways lately. I keep falling in love with Him over and over again.

Chapter 25

Everyday Miracles

4/8/95: Palm Sunday. Palm Sunday service was good. I don't have the words to express how I feel. The chaplain had me help serve the Lord's Supper. What an honor! Each heart, each soul, with such different desires, needs and dreams. Yet there is one answer for each: Jesus Christ, the Son of God. I looked in each person's eyes. I saw longing, love, need, joy and sadness. Oh, just a touch from my Savior. It's been a long journey, but for this moment in time, this is my family—women who all want to be elsewhere, women I've come to love and care about, my sisters in Christ. Oh, how I fought accepting those around me.

Yes, just a touch from my Savior. I knew the power of His touch. Not only had He touched me, He was making a miracle of me—a thoroughly changed woman, from the inside out. What He had done in my life was a miracle, and it was a miracle that, given the woman I had been two-and-a-half years earlier, I could celebrate with all my heart on Easter Sunday.

4/15/95: Easter Sunday. What a great morning! Yes, I am still in a federal prison, but I have been with Jesus. The day was just coming alive. We had special permission to have a sunrise service outside. We all gathered around as the chaplain read from Matthew. Then we gathered in a huge circle (about 150 women—all colors, all classes, all ages—standing together). My heart was flooded with the thought of how all barriers come down in Jesus. I was moved by the sight of unity in diversity and by the desperation in each woman. Oh, when you ask to see through His eyes, it will happen.

The Holy Spirit continued to daily awaken my heart to more of His presence and His power and led me into an unusual season of revelation. Sometimes He revealed Himself in ways that seemed spectacular, and at other times, He was completely pragmatic. That Easter Sunday evening the Spirit revealed another, totally different, aspect of His unlimited self to me:

4/15/95: Oh, to listen to our hearts! I learned a great lesson today. We were watching a video. I started it in a small chapel classroom and then had to move to another. No plugs worked. I tried the library. No plugs in the library worked. I didn't have my I.D. to check out another tape player. Nothing went my *way. But I see how all of that dug into some areas that needed cleaning out in my heart. I asked for forgiveness, repented and then asked the Holy Spirit to empower me to overcome the way I reacted inside. I've learned that I cannot make any of these heart changes. I must lean on the Spirit. Now, I look forward to my next "inconvenience" so I can know the power of God in this area of my life.*

The Holy Spirit was teaching me about His power in so many of its various forms, showing me that it could be manifested just as mightily in gentleness as in force, that something as soft as a raindrop could be just as powerful as claps of thunder and bolts of lightening. I just had to learn to recognize the many facets of His power, to see them for the acts of God that they were.

None of these things I experienced, to the casual observer, would have seemed especially remarkable or have appeared to be works of spectacular might. But they were. The Holy Spirit was showing me the quiet side of power, reminding me that *any* work He does in the hearts of people is a sign and a wonder. And I wondered what tender miracle He would show me next.

> *4/21/95: Each week it seems that the Holy Spirit is drawing me closer. I am understanding and "seeing" so much every day. In Ben's class this week, I saw the power of humility as Ben stepped aside so that the Holy Spirit could minister through an inmate. Ben said that the Holy Spirit didn't want a one-man show. He wants to use everyone. The Holy Spirit flooded the room with His presence.*

Part of the Holy Spirit's rhythm as He taught me was that He would show me a truth in His Word, or put it on undeniable display (as in the case of Ben's demonstration of humility) and then give me an opportunity to practice what I had learned. Less than two weeks passed before I had a chance to experience and exercise humility during one of our church services.

> *5/2/95: Sunday communion was so powerful. We laid our burdens on the Lord. Then we exchanged the elements of*

communion with someone. I was with Kaye. We said to each other, "I need your help," and then prayed for one another. It was as if I had Kaye's heart. I actually felt the burden she carries for her children and her husband. Tears were flowing.

I—the self-sufficient, confident woman who thrived on independence—had looked another person in the eye and said, "I need your help." Those words had never escaped my lips before. I would have interrupted them as a sign of weakness, but no longer. As I spoke them, I could feel their force—the power of humility.

In addition to everything else the Spirit was showing me, I also saw afresh the truly awesome, life-changing power of the Word. Yes, I was confined to a place where my natural eyes looked upon the same dingy, drab surroundings all day long, every day of the year. But in the Lord, I always had something to watch. He revealed Himself in a million creative ways: touching the hearts of women, speaking to us through guest ministers, answering prayer, healing and delivering and a host of other everyday miracles. Day after day, I watched Him set captives free, and May 10, 1995 was no exception.

5/10/95: I just saw the power of 1 John 1:9 manifested! A burdened soul confessed and was freed. Belinda was hiding a painful secret from her past—afraid to tell anyone. We talked in her room and then went to the mop closet where the Spirit blessed us with His sweet presence. Glory. Her eyes sparkled as tears ran down her cheeks. The simple truth—freeing a burdened soul by the power of the Word.

During my incarceration, the Holy Spirit had taught me so much. One thing I learned was that the Spirit and the

Word work together. If I were not grounded in the Word and only tried to hear subjectively from the Spirit, I could be easily deceived. If I only tried to understand and obey the Word without the Holy Spirit, I would be dry and lifeless. I wanted a balanced life.

The Spirit showed me a vision one day, revealing this truth in a way I could understand. I saw a moving sidewalk, like the ones in airports. He drew my attention to the two hand-rails, and said, "Mary, always hold on to both." I immediately knew what He meant. I was to "hold on" to both the Word and the Spirit.

The Word and the Spirit together, guiding my life. Staying grounded in the Word; staying free in the Spirit—that was my commitment. And I loved watching the Word and the Spirit work together. That combination is unbeatable and always victorious. I saw it at work during one of Herman's meetings when, after he taught from the Bible, the Holy Spirit revealed Himself in a powerful way.

6/5/95: Nothing short of a visit from heaven. Herman just "had a chat" with us. He simply taught the Word. Then he began to pray at the end. The Spirit fell all over us.

Then Mattie needed prayer. We joined together in the prayer closet off of the chapel. The Holy Spirit was totally in control as Charlotte prayed. Then Charlotte requested that we pray for Bill, which we did. But God had more in mind. (I believe that God always has more in mind.) I prayed for Bill, then prayed for healing for Charlotte. I touched Charlotte's forehead and down she went. I prayed for those old wounds that He showed me Saturday night.

Then the Spirit began pouring over me, washing me, cleansing me and filling me. I couldn't move. I just stood, weeping as He encouraged me. I sensed God's holiness for a moment. I could do nothing but cry out to Him, "Cleanse me! Change me! Take away my will and give me Yours!"

Oh, how I love Jesus! No words can really describe.

Through the end of the summer, the Spirit continued to show me places in my heart that needed to be touched by His power—areas of my heart that were not healed, not whole.

7/9/95: What can I say? The Holy Spirit revealed a burden I was carrying—shame of the past. He led me through the "great exchange of the cross," showing me that Jesus took my shame and gave me glory. I had prayed for healing right before church and He answered my prayer.

I marveled at His microscopic knowledge of my life, at His ability to highlight and heal a part of my heart I did not even know was damaged. Now *that* was power! I marveled, too, at the persistence of His power to bring change in my life. He simply refused to leave me in the condition I was in.

8/9/95: What a night in the Lord I've had. It is a great moment when the Holy Spirit takes the light of His Word and penetrates your heart. Even though there is pain, there is joy. Even though there is sadness, there is freedom. The Holy Spirit showed me my heart. It was bad. I wept and asked forgiveness for not walking in love. Something happened tonight.

Something was always happening in my walk with the Holy Spirit. I rejoiced that He never left me the way I was but always called me to go deeper and higher at the same time. During mid-August 1995, the enemy began trying to bring division in some of my Christian friendships. I knew that I had to gain the Lord's perspective on my friendships and asked the Spirit to help me understand what was happening.

> *8/18/95: I have been asking the Lord why I felt so distant from my friends lately. He told me it was because I hadn't been trusting them. And that I didn't really think they cared for me. I gave, but I did not receive from them (due to my attitude). I repented and asked God to change me. I felt love pass between us. I am free. I am free.*

What a miracle. His power, in just some of its infinite variety, had set me free. Stuck behind bars, confined to a federal prison, I was free.

I reveled in the freedom the Holy Spirit had brought to my heart and mind, but I wanted my outside to catch up with my inside! I wanted to go home and longed for my release, never sure when it would take place, never sure when I would hear anything about it. And so, the Holy Spirit showed me yet another aspect of power, not so much His power to do anything, but His power to enable *me* to do something by His grace—to exercise the power to wait and the power to trust.

Chapter 26

Believing Anyway

Prisoners are people too. They feel. They hurt. They get tired. They get lonely. And they get cancer. That happened to my friend Robbie—a striking African-American woman, in her late twenties, who lived two cells down the hall from me. She had beautiful, thick, black hair and a bright, contagious smile that reflected the cheer inside of her. Even though she was separated from her two young children, she did not "wear" the heaviness that most other lonely mothers did, but greeted the rigors of prison life with a positive attitude.

At one point, I noticed that Robbie was watching me. For weeks, she said little, but seemed to be studying my life. I was sitting on my bunk reading one day when I heard someone come into my cell and glanced up to see Robbie walking toward me with her Bible in hand. Before I could even say "hello," she plopped down beside me and said, "Okay, what do I do?"

Although she was a Christian, she had not spent much time in the Word. But that day, I could tell by the look in her eye that she meant business with the Lord. She was ready to see change in her life, and I was thrilled.

I pointed to the Bible in her lap and said, "Well, the Old Testament is on the left. The New Testament is on the right. And Jesus is in the middle." That was the starting point, and from there I went on to share with her many things the Holy Spirit had taught me. It was the beginning of another God-appointed friendship, a unique relationship that would impact each of us profoundly, but in radically different ways.

Robbie's situation was particularly urgent. Unlike so many inmates, she was not counting the days until she got out of prison and went home. She was in prison living out the last days of her life—but no one knew, not even Robbie.

The Holy Spirit awakened me one night with an unusual instruction—to go stand in the bathroom. *Why do You want me to go stand in the bathroom?* I asked silently. *It's the middle of the night!* But I knew He had spoken, so I crawled out of my bunk, wrapped my coat-of-many-colors around me and shuffled down the hall in my flip-flops.

I walked into the bathroom, looked around and saw nothing out of the ordinary. I stood. I waited. I felt so ridiculous and wondered whether I had actually heard the Holy Spirit or not.

When I checked with Him, He spoke again and said "Wait," so I continued to stand in the bathroom. After several minutes, Robbie stumbled in and before I knew it, collapsed in my arms. I was in perfect position to catch her, but because I was not expecting her sudden fall, both of us tumbled to the floor.

I screamed for a guard. "I need an officer in the bathroom! It's an emergency! I need an officer in here now!" I then began to do everything I could think of—took her pulse, checked her breathing and looked at her pupils. When the guard arrived, he had no idea how to help her and immediately radioed for the physician's assistant, Mrs. Cohen. When she arrived, she stated her intended course of action: first, phenergan tablets.

"No," I insisted. "Not tablets. Use a suppository."

She looked at me in total disbelief, but knew I was right. Then, I began to tell her which tests needed to be run and to order a stretcher immediately because Robbie needed to be transported to the medical unit right away.

My pharmaceutical training never prepared me to give the medical instructions I blurted out that night. Clinical terms I did not even understand rolled off my tongue with perfect confidence and ease. I had no natural knowledge of what to do, yet I knew exactly what to do. Mrs. Cohen normally would never have listened to me (or any other inmate), but she followed my directions precisely. It was a moment when the Holy Spirit completely took over a situation, a prime example of Luke 12:12, "For the Holy Spirit will teach you in that very hour what you ought to say."

Several days after that incident, we learned that Robbie was sick—very sick. There was talk that she had cancer. Whatever she had was serious enough for her to be transferred to a prison in Ft. Worth—one that had a specialized medical facility.

Prior to her move, I witnessed one of the most stunning and tender acts of compassion I have ever seen. With a dull pair of round-tipped scissors (the only kind allowed in prison), Robbie cut off her beautiful black hair. As chunks of it floated to the floor, she explained that she did not want the other cancer patients at the hospital to feel bad when they saw her full head of hair while they had none.

Of course, no one knew when Robbie would be transferred to the medical facility for treatment, but at some seemingly random moment, a guard would show up at her cell and within minutes, she and her belongings would be gone. It happened all the time. A long-awaited transfer would finally come through, and people who had become friends would be forced to make a quick and final exit from our lives. Many times, we did not have a chance to say good-bye, to wish a woman well, or to bring any type of closure to a kind of friendship only fellow prisoners understand.

One morning my name appeared on the call-out sheet, and I saw that I was scheduled for a medical visit. *Why?* I wondered. I had never requested an appointment with a doctor. But I was required to go, and when I arrived, the medical staff had no knowledge—not even a notation on their records—of an appointment for me that day. My name was not on their list, so I went back to my cell completely baffled.

Because of the unexplainable order that sent me to the infirmary, I missed the morning van to MHMR. Another van would not be going until after lunch that day, so I had several hours to fill, and decided to visit Robbie in her cell. I sat on her bunk and we talked for about two hours. We shared so many things that were in our hearts, and I prayed for her before I left to catch the van for MHMR.

I went to work at 1:00 that afternoon and returned to the dorm around 3:30. Robbie was gone. She had been transferred during the two hours since I had seen her. All I could think was, *He knew.* God knew Robbie was leaving that afternoon, though she didn't and I didn't. He gave me such a special gift of time with her—a gift of time we needed together as friends. He is amazing. There is nothing He does not know, and His timing is absolutely perfect.

I had to trust His timing, not only in Robbie's life, but also in my own. One afternoon during the summer of 1995, I was summoned to a "team meeting," which meant that my "team" (the group of prison officials assigned to manage my case and oversee my prison term) had something to report. Consistent with the nature of prison, I did not know the purpose of the meeting. It could have been anything, with any number of unpleasant consequences. But the Lord was in charge. He was orchestrating my life and had arranged for me to hear good news that day.

> *6/21/95: What a day. What surprises my Father has! I was called into team tonight. I thought it was early. Well, the shock came. I have about 23 months to go, including halfway house and house arrest time. I'll be eligible to apply for a furlough and for work release. I was stunned.*
>
> *I joined Kaye and Charlotte on the track to share my joy. Tears came flowing as they hugged me. They are both scheduled to leave way before me, so they rejoiced with me over the light at the end of my tunnel. We went to the benches surrounding the track to praise God together. I am still in shock. Time to seek the face of my Father even more.*

The end of my prison stay was finally in sight and not only that, I actually had a vague sense of what my remaining twenty-three months might entail: I could be granted a furlough, of twelve, twenty-four or thirty-six hours, depending on the team's decision. The prison officials were also considering me for a work-release program, which meant that I could move out of the prison and complete that portion of my sentence living in a halfway house and working at a job wherever I was assigned. I hoped the furlough would be approved and that the team would indeed try to arrange a work-release for me. Two days later, I had answers.

> *6/23/95: My team went well. They approved my furlough and agreed to send off a request for work-release! It's time. It's a change of seasons for me. All I can think about is God's kindness and mercy! And I think about my true friends—people who have enriched my life and those He has allowed me to help. It is such a privilege to serve Jesus. Jesus! Jesus! I thought of Matthew 6:33, "But seek first the kingdom of God and His righteousness, and all these things shall be added to you."*

As I had written in my journal, I did think often about my true friends, many of whom I would be leaving forever when my release came. And when I thought of friends, I always thought of Robbie.

The summer of 1995 passed with occasional news of her condition—and it was never good. We prayed and prayed, asking God to heal her. But one day, the chaplain, who stayed in touch with the medical facility in Ft. Worth, informed us that Robbie had died. "No!" my heart revolted. It could not be! Not our tenderhearted, happy Robbie!

But it was true. She did die, and her death sent my faith into its most severe crisis. I struggled to understand how Robbie could die after so many faith-filled prayers and as I did, the Holy Spirit reminded me that it was my job to pray and believe, but God's job to answer prayer—and that He sometimes responded in ways that defied my understanding. I knew that Robbie was healed ultimately, and instantly, when she entered the presence of the Lord, but I never understood why she was not healed before she died. Nothing builds trust in the Lord like a lack of understanding.

Chapter 27

The Healer

My experience with Robbie did not change the truth that the Lord does heal people, and when I went to prison, I did not know that. I had seen Vincent use crystals to relieve a woman's headache, so perhaps I knew that some sort of healing power existed in the supernatural realm, but I also knew that what I saw that night was from the dark side and not of the Lord.

One day, within the first few months of my arrival at Benton, the Holy Spirit spoke to me and told me to go into the television room and turn on a certain channel. When I did, I saw a preacher who said that the Lord heals. Just as I had been with Vincent and his crystals, I was intrigued. The preacher simply opened his Bible and read scriptures that pointed to the healing provided by Jesus' death on the cross. He then asked people who were sick to place a hand on any diseased or injured part of their body. I put my hand on my right foot, the one that had been diagnosed with a tumor before my trial. As the preacher prayed, I believed that the Lord would heal me.

Within several days, the pain in my foot disappeared and did not return.

Any healing is a miracle, but what was remarkable to me was that I could believe in it. Until I went to prison, I had always leaned on medicine as my first and only recourse for anything from a headache to pneumonia, and it never occurred to me to ask the Lord to heal me or anyone else. My ability to embrace the truth of divine healing was a paradigm shift of the first order!

The Holy Spirit led me specifically to three scriptures that helped me understand God's provision for healing. I read Deuteronomy 28, which taught me that sickness can be a curse that results from disobeying the Lord. But He also took me to Galatians 3:13, "Christ has redeemed us from the curse of the law, having become a curse for us (for it is written, 'Cursed is everyone who hangs on a tree')." That was awesome—the curse of disease and infirmity had been paid for, nailed to the cross with Jesus! The Holy Spirit also showed me 1 Peter 2:24, which says that Jesus is the one "by whose stripes you *were* healed" (italics mine). I hadn't realized this truth before—that when Jesus died on the cross to forgive sin, He also purchased healing.

His work transformed everything about me, every aspect of my life in spirit, soul and body. As I experienced healing personally, I also began to pray for other people to be healed. We prisoners did not have the luxury of running to the local drugstore or supermarket to pick up a prescription or a pain reliever, so I had plenty of opportunities to share and exercise my faith in His healing power.

One of the first people I saw actually minister healing to others was Betty, the minister who held services on Thursday nights. The Lord used her to lay hands on sick women, and He healed them. As I watched her, I was encouraged and my faith grew. Betty only came once a week, but women were sick all the time and were rarely able to obtain adequate medical care. I knew that the Holy Spirit's healing ministry did not only flow through Betty, but that others could also pray for the sick and believe God for their recovery. I wrote about one of my own early experiences in my journal:

6/30/94: Last night Glenda passed out in the common area. I ran down right at count time. Her eyes were rolling back in her head and she couldn't breathe. Guards came with a stretcher. I walked out with them and Glenda on the stretcher as they waited for the cart to carry her to medical. I laid hands on her and prayed out loud as the guards held on to the stretcher. Glenda is up and hungry this morning. She is weak, but okay. Thank You, Jesus. (The guards from last night looked at me so funny this morning, but I felt no shame.)

Word seemed to fly at lightning speed when women began to hear that the Lord was healing other inmates, so praying for the sick became a regular part of my life. Sometimes the women who asked for prayer were friends, and sometimes they were women, like Vanessa, whom I hardly knew.

2/15/95: Last night I prayed with Vanessa for her daughter's healing. Vanessa thought she would have to have a hysterectomy, but when she went to the doctor, she said he only "looked around" and did not operate. Glory to God!

Before long, Betty allowed several inmates, including me, to help her pray for people during her meetings. The more I prayed for people, the more I learned to cooperate with the Holy Spirit in His healing ministry.

3/18/95: A woman went up to Betty for prayer. She was unable to raise her hands. Betty asked me to lay hands on the woman as she prayed. My hands were hot, and the woman said she could feel her back getting hot too as God's power touched and healed her. Then she was able to raise her hands with no pain.

Sometimes we could discern the source of a person's problem quickly; sometimes we could not. At one of Ben's meetings, I knew immediately that a woman was oppressed by an evil spirit, specifically, a deaf spirit.

3/19/95: Today's service was good. At the end, Ben was praying for Jennifer. He asked me to come up. There was a deaf spirit oppressing her. I sensed the Holy Spirit telling me to stick my fingers in her ears and she fell down and was baptized with the Holy Spirit.

3/21/95: I saw Jennifer as she was coming in from the doctor. He said it was earwax.

We knew better. We appreciated physicians and regarded them as vessels through which God's healing power often flowed. We were glad Jennifer had been to the doctor, but all along, we had been praying for her, believing the Word and trusting Him to heal her.

One day, sickness hit particularly close to home. After struggling with some unexplainable vision problems, Liz paid a visit to the physician's assistant, who diagnosed a tumor on her eye muscle. As soon as she shared this news with the Remnant Group, we began to pray that the Lord would heal her. Meanwhile, someone in the prison infirmary had scheduled her to see an outside physician. When that time came, we were confident that the Lord had answered our prayers and eager for the doctor to confirm the miracle.

7/2/95: Liz went to a doctor on the outside Wednesday. She had been diagnosed with a tumor on the eye muscle. We prayed in the van that today would be the day her healing would manifest. When she saw the doctor on Wednesday, there was no tumor!

Perhaps the most dramatic healing occurred with a woman named Shantel, who had been told that she was going blind.

10/8/95: Last night when I arrived in my cell, Maggie, my cellmate, told me that Shantel had patches on her eyes. I went to check on her. Holy anger arose in me as I remembered that Shantel had just recently told me how the Lord had healed her last week. She had a severe infection in her eyes. The enemy was trying to steal her vision and her testimony. They told her she was going to lose her vision and go blind. I laid hands on her, and the power of God went through her. This morning the physician's assistant took the patches off and she could see! No infection! She testified today of her healing.

I could not have been happier. I loved seeing the power of the enemy cancelled and the power of God turn a situation around.

What a miracle! A former pharmacist praying for fellow inmates and seeing them healed—more evidence of how much I had been changed. I wrote in my journal about one particular incident involving medicine:

Came in from Ben's class and I saw two ibuprofen on the table. Maggie said she had a headache. I got my oil, anointed

her, laid hands on her and prayed. We talked a few min-
utes and she said, "It's gone!" Oh how truly my heart has
changed! My first response was Jesus—a long way from
my pharmacy days.

I also discovered that healing was not limited to the physical realm, but that people could be as sick or wounded in
their emotions and minds as they were in their bodies. Far
more prevalent than physical illness was a condition that can
cause even greater damage: a broken heart.

I encountered many women who had been abandoned,
suffered horrible abuse or been otherwise mistreated, and I
met women who had never overcome the deep disappointments their lives had dealt them. They lived with the symptoms of brokenheartedness—anger, fear, insecurity, bitterness,
depression and fragmented personalities. Unforgiveness ran
through their veins like poison. Truly, these women needed
to be healed and made whole.

One of the most brokenhearted women I ever met was
Beatrice, whose heart had been shattered by the pain and
guilt of two abortions. She was new at Benton and had attended our Bible study for several weeks, but I did not know
her well. When she came into my cell and asked for prayer, I
knew that she was carrying a deep secret—something she
had never told anyone.

I introduced her to the mop closet, which was filled with
an unusually strong odor that night, and both of us took a
seat on the floor, using a dust mop as a cushion. Sobbing as
she shared her story, she verbalized for the first time in her
life the shame and condemnation and deep remorse she felt
over having the abortions. The weight of the guilt had crushed
her, and she simply could not live with it anymore.

I opened my Bible to 1 John 1:9 and pointed out each power-packed word to her: "If we confess our sins, He is faithful and just to forgive us our sins and to cleanse us from all unrighteousness." She kept crying, so I kept reading that verse over and over again to her.

"Beatrice," I said, "You've confessed your sin! God is faithful to forgive you and to wash all this guilt off of you. You don't have to carry the burden anymore!"

We prayed and she received the Lord's forgiveness, which allowed her then to forgive herself. The Holy Spirit showed her a vision—a picture of her babies in heaven. The process of receiving His forgiveness, forgiving herself and knowing that her children were with the Lord began an incredible healing work in her heart and over time allowed her to gain inner strength and wholeness she had never known before.

I met with women who had been sexually abused or physically beaten—or both—and with women who had done heinous things to their own children. All of them were in unbearable emotional pain and sometimes they didn't even know it. I remember one woman who came and asked me to pray for relief from a toothache, but we ended up dealing with the impact of her being abused for eight years by her step-father.

I knew the Holy Spirit wanted to heal the hearts of all these women and that He had a specific healing journey mapped out for each one. I could not heal them; I could only do my best to help them follow Him.

9/21/95: The Lord is taking me to people with such deep emotional wounds—so many old wounds. Healing takes more than the laying on of hands. Much wisdom is needed to help them.

As I continued to pray about the larger issue of

brokenheartedness and emotional healing, the Holy Spirit spoke to me and gave me insight into some of the dynamics of a wounded heart.

> *9/28/95: The Lord told me that many people have deep wounds and try to heal them with an outside bandage. It's like putting a new, pretty shoe on a broken foot and thinking that since it looks better, it really is better. Well, the Spirit must be allowed to "enter that area" of a person's life to cleanse, heal and repair. Then strength will come. So much to know and understand. Only God can heal these wounds.*

Yes, only God. Only God, by the power of the Holy Spirit, could do these fresh, new works of healing and wholeness and restoration, and yet this healing power was the work of the ages, a ministry that Jesus Himself both performed and spoke of: "The Spirit of the Lord is upon Me, because He has anointed Me to preach the gospel to the poor; He has sent Me to heal the brokenhearted, to proclaim liberty to the captives and recovery of sight to the blind, to set at liberty those who are oppressed; to proclaim the acceptable year of the Lord" (Luke 4:18, 19).

The power of Jesus' ministry described in those Bible verses had transformed my life. I needed every element of it: the hearing of the true gospel message, the healing of a broken heart, freedom from the bondage in my soul, the ability to see things clearly and the assurance of God's love and favor toward me. His ministry had changed me, yet it was still changing me and the passionate cry of my heart became, "Father, do for others what You've done for me." I wanted Him to make Luke 4:18 and 19 as real in the lives of other people as He had in mine— and I was watching Him do it, one woman at a time.

Chapter 28

Not Against Flesh and Blood

"For we do not wrestle against flesh and blood, but against principalities, against powers, against the rulers of the darkness of this age, against spiritual hosts of wickedness in the heavenly places" (Ephesians 6:12). Early in my prison stay, someone gave me a book that ripped the veil in my mind between the visible world and the invisible world. *This Present Darkness* opened my eyes in an intensely practical way to the reality of the spiritual realm and to the fact that nothing happens on earth that heaven is not aware of or involved in. Reading that book was like looking through binoculars into a region beyond the natural realm and being able to actually watch the war between angels and demons. It was like witnessing the constant conflict that manifests on earth through everyday situations in people's lives—the conflict of two kingdoms, the kingdom of darkness and the Kingdom of light.

After I read the book, and as I continued to meditate on Ephesians 6:12, I began to be able to identify the evidence of evil influences in my life and in situations around me. As I became aware of these unseen forces, I realized that demons, evil spirits, had been influencing and oppressing me all of my life. *How could this be?* I wondered.

During my childhood and teenage years, I had been what most people would consider a "good girl." Nothing about me would have indicated that invisible spirits were busy designing my destruction—and using me to accomplish it! But once I got to prison and began my journey with the Holy Spirit, He opened my eyes to the fact that evil spirits afflict all kinds of people.

When Gary visited me, I knew that "something" had left me when he commanded it to leave, and I knew that it had been something vile and vicious. Since that time, I had experienced other instances of deliverance from evil spirits, each one resulting in a noticeable increase of peace and clarity and inner freedom in my life. I also saw many bizarre, unexplainably horrible things in prison, things that were undeniably demonic. My personal experience with deliverance, study of the Word and observance of so much unmistakable evil convinced me beyond any doubt that as surely as God's angels existed, so did the devil's demons. I knew that I had to deal with demonic activity by walking in the same spiritual authority I had seen Gary exercise, and I had read about in Luke 10:19, "Behold, I give you the authority to trample on serpents and scorpions, *and over all the power of the enemy,* and nothing shall by any means hurt you" (italics mine).

As always, the Holy Spirit was faithful to teach me how to follow Jesus' example as I learned how to minister His freedom to women who lived under the relentless tyranny of those invisible enemies. Just as the Lord gave me many opportunities to pray for women who needed physical and emotional healing, He also led me to pray for people who needed deliverance from demonic powers. One of my most fervent longings was to see people released from the enemy's clutches, and I rejoiced every time his power was broken and God's power freed people. I wrote one journal entry after another about the awesome miracles I saw the Holy Spirit work as He took away their pain, gave them peace and began to make tormented, fragmented women whole and strong and free.

But a person must use wisdom and discernment in the realm of the miraculous and be careful not to walk in presumption. I knew from John 5:19 and John 8:26, 28 that Jesus only did what He saw His Father do and did not operate apart from His Father's direction. One afternoon, in my zeal to be a vessel through which signs and wonders could flow, I presumed the Spirit wanted to use me to minister deliverance and realized later that I did not ask Him first before jumping into a frightening situation.

4/1/95: I had a peaceful morning with Jesus. When I walked in the dorm, Greta and Sandy stopped me and told me that Becky was twirling in her room with one hand over her eyes, in the dark. She was blowing air out of her mouth and then sucking it back in. I went to her cell, yelling, "Becky! Becky!" She didn't acknowledge me. I pled the blood of Jesus and bound the spirit. I turned on the light. No response. She clawed me with the hand that was not covering her eyes, bending my hand back and scratching my arm with her fingernails. She was totally out of control.

Officer Wellington came running up the stairs as the spirit was trying to throw Becky and me down the stairs, but Jean pulled Becky back. It was time for 10:00 A.M. count, so guards came from everywhere. They tried to restrain her in the bathroom. The spirit began to scream, but then Becky began to scream, "I believe in the Lord Jesus Christ! Satan, I rebuke you in Jesus' Name!" Then the spirit would start screaming again—a loud shrill scream. It took six officers to hold her down.

The chaplain came at 10:40 and tried to talk to Becky. At times, Becky knew her and said, "Chap, pray for me!" Then the awful screams would start again. Finally, using a bed sheet, they carried her out the emergency exit. An officer ordered me to the infirmary to get treated for the scratches on my hand. I had to go.

I can't totally express what happened today. I moved in presumption. I am humbled again. I saw tears well up in Officer Wellington's eyes after they took Becky away. She told me she's seen this before and that people can't push God to move in their timing and that the Holy Spirit is the one who must do the teaching.

As sobering as the experience with Becky was, I could not let it keep me from ministering deliverance—I just had to be sure I ministered only as the Holy Spirit led me. I had learned an important lesson about presumption but before long wrote in my journal about a wonderful experience with His delivering power:

5/20/95: Just got in from prayer meeting. As we prayed the Holy Spirit said, "Pray for Nancy." I asked her if she wanted her prayer language. She stood. I prayed. She went down. Then she began to cough. We prayed some more. She told us something was in her throat. As I was praying, she grabbed my hand and placed it on the back of her neck. I knew it was the Spirit showing me what to do. When it was all over, Nancy just wept and bowed before Jesus.

The Holy Spirit never ceased to amaze me as He drew people out of the misery of oppression and bondage into freedom and wholeness. Just as my experience with Becky had been dramatic in a negative way, I had an equally dramatic experience with my friend, Maria, and its outcome was marvelous:

7/22/95: Last night's Remnant Group was incredible. Maria said even before dinner, "I'm expecting something great tonight." I remembered praying as I walked over, prompted by the Spirit, "Lord, give us the right room tonight." Before everyone got there (with just Beatrice and Charlotte) I prayed for the blood of Jesus to be a covering for our meeting and asked the angels to stand guard. As we began to gather, we walked around singing to the Lord for a bit, then had communion.

After everyone had arrived, Charlotte sensed as she was praying that someone was confused, so she asked who had confusion. Maria, Sylvia and Beatrice stood. Maria walked over to me and said, "Mary, it is calling me 'Stupid. Stupid.'" I began to take authority over the evil spirit, binding its work, rebuking it and commanding it to leave Maria in Jesus' name. I had no idea what we were about to go through.

The spirit spoke and said, "No, I won't leave. I've been here a long time." The Holy Spirit guided me. I commanded the spirit to be silent. Maria shook violently on the floor, slithering backwards and shaking her head. An officer peeked in the room about 8:30. I motioned for him to leave, and he did.

At one point, Maria became limp. We thought the evil spirit had left her and that the whole ordeal was over.

Well, it was not over. During the time she was lying limply on the floor, the spirit had spoken to her again, saying, "I fooled them. I fooled them." (She told me that this morning.) After a few minutes' rest, it started again. At times, Maria could not even talk. What a battle! The whole thing took 45 minutes. At 8:50, we thought the demon left her. Maria was drained. We walked her into the dorm to her cell.

This morning she is very sore but thinks clearly. This reminded me of the 70 people in Luke 10 who returned to Jesus rejoicing that demons were subject to them in His name. Jesus told them to rejoice instead that their names were written in the Lamb's Book of Life.

I had a feeling that the Holy Spirit had only begun the work in Maria and that there was more to come. But I was surprised at how quickly He resumed His work in her:

7/23/95: Sunday at dinner I ate with Maria, Nancy and Maggie. We'd just gotten started and Maria had to leave because she felt sick. I waited a moment, then the Holy Spirit said, "Go." I caught up with her and she was under attack. She couldn't even speak. We went into the mop room. "It" was manifesting again. I prayed and we praised, pleading the blood of Jesus. Maria's body seemed to bounce about four inches off the ground. It left. Maria and I rejoiced in the mop room, praising God. And Maria was not even sore! It was amazing.

It was *all* amazing to me—the Holy Spirit's unique way of bringing freedom to each person in ways that she could best receive it. In many cases, but not always, visible manifestations accompanied deliverance ministry. When I ministered to two inmates, Darlene and Melissa, both of them exhibited outward signs of demons leaving, but I believed some oppression left me as well, in a quiet, peaceful, invisible way.

> *4/13/96: Victory in Jesus!! I am on cloud 100! So much to tell. Major event prayer meeting. Jesus delivered Darlene and Melissa! When Melissa came in late for the meeting, the Holy Spirit's presence was so heavy that she hit her knees immediately. Then she felt sick and ran outside. She came back in and fell to her knees. Darlene felt sick too. We took authority over the spirit in Melissa. She shook and thrashed and growled. She coughed something up. Darlene also went down and coughed something out.*
>
> *Then we sang victory songs! Glory! I felt I was set free too. It was incredible to see God at work. He was so real tonight. He allowed me to see His glory. The anointing destroys the yoke of the enemy.*

One of the most wonderful things about everything I experienced and learned in prison was that the Lord wanted to use me to minister His power to people around me. Ministering freedom from demonic oppression is not for the few, but for all who believe. It is part of normal Christianity, and it flows naturally out of our connection to Jesus, who lives to set the captives free.

Chapter 29

The Announcement

I would have recognized the handwriting anywhere. I had seen it a million times, but not in many months. Shocked and curious, I looked at the letter I had just received at mail call. It was from Mike—and it was another piece of correspondence I would not read in the presence of other inmates, but took straight to the refuge of a bathroom stall.

The matter had been settled months ago; we were finished. *Why is he contacting me now?* I wondered. *What could he possibly have to say? Is there something left undone?* A surprise flicker of hope flared up in my heart. Was the relationship I had "cast upon the waters" returning? Even though I truly believed that Mike and I were not meant to be together and had done my best to completely release him, in the far corners of my mind, I still wondered. As hard as I tried to ignore them, questions lurked like cobwebs in an empty house: Would it work out after all? Could the break in our relationship be only temporary?

I read Mike's lengthy letter. He wrote about his life—a new church he had joined in Ft. Worth; a woman he had dated, but broken up with a couple of months ago; a local children's home to which he was generous with both his time and his financial resources. The best thing about the children's home, he wrote, was that God was using it to heal his loss of the baby. With a prick in my own heart, I thanked the Lord for that. The letter ended with a request for me to call him on a certain Saturday morning at a certain time. He would be waiting.

Nervous and barely able to breathe, I dialed his number at the appointed time and placed a collect call to the only man I ever gave my heart to, the man whose voice I had not heard in months. We exchanged a few formalities and stumbled through the first several minutes of our conversation with the kind of awkwardness that only exists between two people who once spoke intimately. But gradually, we began to converse with greater ease.

Our phone visit seemed to be drawing to a cordial close, and then Mike made a staggering statement: "Mary, I want to come see you." I froze. I could not talk for several seconds that seemed like hours. Then, I felt as though my emotions had been dumped into a blender and turned on "high." Did I want to see him again after all this time? I just did not know. I could not decide. But, in the end, I agreed to let him come to visit a few weeks later.

> *4/22/95: I called Mike at 8:45. I am being so prayerful about all of this. We talked for one hour and fifteen minutes because no other inmates were waiting to use the phone, screaming "Limit!" and making me get off after ten minutes. I heard the spark in his voice and knew he took in all I said as I shared how God has changed my heart, how I've had to learn God's ways.*
>
> *We both have a lot to ponder. I don't know if this is "going" anywhere. I wonder if he realizes how different I am—free,*

not bound or controlled by evil spirits—now under the control of Jesus. Glory to God. I've spent the day very quiet. Thinking, remembering. I know He will guide each heart. Reconciliation? Seems impossible. Could this be God?

I wavered between thinking reconciliation really was impossible—out of the question—and thinking the Lord could actually be restoring our relationship. For the next three weeks my thoughts bounced from "it's impossible" to "this is going to work after all" and everywhere in between. I could only wait. And I could take care of the one practical concern I needed to address before his visit—re-submitting his name to the authorities responsible for the visiting lists.

One of the most painful decisions I made in prison was to remove Mike's name from my list of approved visitors. But I *had* to. When I relinquished our relationship, I knew I had to sever all ties with him. I remembered the agony—like I was cutting myself in two. My parents lived too far away to visit me regularly, so Mike really was my only lifeline to any place beyond Benton. Without his name on the visiting list, I felt not only isolated from him; I felt isolated from the whole world.

Unsure whether I really wanted to put his name back on my list or not, I did. That was the only way we could see each other; and I had to give us one last chance.

When the day of Mike's visit arrived, I awakened extra early, showered, tried to blow-dry a little bit of curl into my hair and carefully applied what make-up I had. An hour before visiting time started, I looked my very best and sat down on my bunk and just waited until I heard, "Forsythe, you've got a visitor" over the P.A. system.

But I never heard those words. Hour after anxious hour, I checked my hair, re-applied my commissary lipstick and sat in my cell anticipating my pre-arranged visit.

But Mike never came.

In fact, I did not hear from him at all. I knew nothing for almost four months. Not another letter, not a phone call. Nothing—until one Saturday night in August when a guard sneered at me as I walked back to my cell from a Remnant Group meeting. "Are you Forsythe?" she asked. Startled, I answered, "Yes, ma'am." She then relayed a message that shot shock waves all the way through me. If my skin had not held me together, I would have fallen apart. Stunned, dazed, I barely managed to comprehend what she said.

Cockily, she informed me that she knew someone I knew, an old girlfriend of Mike's—the one he had been dating until that past January. *This is against the rules*, I thought. *She isn't supposed to be telling me anything about anybody outside! Why is she doing this? Is this just another cruel prison trick?*

As she continued, I realized she knew too much to be lying to me, even though I wanted her story to be untrue. She *did* know Mike's former girlfriend and had heard from her that Mike was getting married.

8/27/95: God is so good. After the meeting Saturday, a guard came up to me and asked, "Are you Forsythe?" She knew someone on the outside who knew me. Laura Simpson, the woman Mike broke up with in January. She told me Laura had phoned her two weeks ago. Mike had called her and said he is getting married.

He was getting married. The question was closed. Finally, I had my answer, but the news hit me with an impact I could not have predicted. It was not a neutral piece of information! After all, Mike and I had spent years together, and we certainly had an unusual history. We had stood shoulder-to-shoulder against formidable foes. We had fought together in the trenches of a legal investigation and a court battle. We had planned a wedding and expected to have a child together. We had suffered the heartache of separation and experienced joint devastation when my pardon was not granted. So much we had shared. Such an intense life together brought to a decisive end for me by an announcement from a prison guard.

Even when I first began to feel the Lord leading me to let him go months previously, a part of me still remained a heart-in-waiting. Until one of us made a commitment to someone else, an ember of hope still smoldered in the ashes of our once-roaring fire. But this piece of news doused that last glowing coal and extinguished forever the wonderings inside of me. It was as devastating to me as the rap of the judge's gavel the day I was found guilty in court.

I continued my journal entry.

> *It was only the Holy Spirit who kept me steady. I did all I could to control my thoughts. My encouragement did not come until after the church service Sunday. The chaplain spoke on "Stay Inside the Gate" and the "gate" is God's will!*
>
> *After church, Charlotte and I prayed and I cried and cried. I haven't told her about Mike yet. I wept because of the deliverance God has given me from the world. Was I remotely thinking of returning to things in the past, like the Israelites? Perhaps, but no more! I know God has a husband waiting who is perfect for the call on my life. I surrendered—again—at His table tonight.*

True, only the Holy Spirit kept me steady when the guard passed along Mike's news, and in the following days, only He helped me regain my sense of balance as I turned my thoughts toward the larger issue of my future. I was not surprised when the Lord sent a little book my way, a book that contained a story that would help me keep loving Him through the pain.

She was a great evangelist, the flaming-haired wearer of flowing gowns, whose fluid movements graced the platforms of auditoriums around the world. She was the enigmatic Kathryn Kuhlman, whose storied life included not only remarkable experiences with God's love and power, but also the raw grief of the soul.

In Kathryn's biography, *Daughter of Destiny*, Jamie Buckingham quoted her as she recalled letting go of the man she loved so that she could fulfill God's call on her life:

> *One afternoon . . . I left the apartment—it was in the outskirts of Los Angeles—and found myself walking down a tree-shaded street. The sun was flickering through the great limbs that stretched out overhead. At the end of the block I saw a street sign. It said simply, "Dead End." There was heartache, heartache so great it cannot be put into words.*[7]

Buckingham continued:

> *Kathryn had known, by the time she was fourteen, that she was destined to be different. Destined to be about her Father's business. It was a feeling she was never able to shake. How, then, could she continue on in a relationship that was not only displeasing to God, but literally preventing her from achieving all that God had planned for her.*[8]

I too had been in a relationship that would have hindered my achieving all that God had planned for me, although I knew little about what that plan would involve. Nevertheless, I had given my heart to Him, and my surrender was complete and unconditional.

Chapter 30

Give and Take

"Happy birthday to you! Happy birthday to you! Happy birthday, dear Mary! Happy birthday to you!"

Ben lent his booming bass voice to a chorus of inmates in a rousing rendition of "Happy Birthday"—and they were all singing to me. Time did not stand still in prison and birthdays came once a year for me just as they did for everyone else, everywhere else.

> 10/3/95: My birthday. At Ben's class tonight, the girls gave me a birthday card and everyone sang to me. It filled my heart with such joy! The friends I have are precious. I even came home to an extra blanket to support my back on my bunk. The Lord's handiwork.

After Ben's class, several friends threw a "surprise" birthday party, prison style, for me. The desire for celebrations always prompted creativity, and long before I ever stepped foot into Benton, someone had figured out how to make banana pudding and had passed down its simple formula from inmate to inmate like a favorite family recipe.

One of my friends donated a medium-sized plastic bowl to the cause, while others pitched in vanilla wafers. Some provided bananas sliced with plastic spoons and others contributed ready-made vanilla pudding. Someone had also taken the time to fill a trash can with ice and placed the pudding on top of it to keep it cold until we returned from Ben's class. All of the ingredients had been purchased at the commissary and meant that each person who participated had given up something for herself so that we could share a few lighthearted moments and enjoy a bowl of banana pudding together.

After the party, when my friends had returned to their cells, I marveled at the team effort that had been exerted and at how much my friends had sacrificed just to be able to give me a special birthday treat.

In addition, I realized that by the time my next birthday rolled around, I would be out of prison. *Wow,* I thought, *I don't know what all the next year of my life will hold, but I'll be able to leave Benton. I won't have to live in a jail cell anymore.* I was not sure where I would go from there, but knew that the next step would take me to another new level of freedom, and I could hardly wait.

A few weeks later, my appreciation for my birthday surprise and anticipation about my upcoming release were interrupted by a sharp reminder of my current reality: birthday or no birthday, I was still a prisoner. And I was still subject to the seemingly senseless and cruel decisions of the prison officials as they relaxed certain restrictions temporarily before clamping down on us again. Within several weeks after my birthday, they changed a policy I appreciated and enjoyed more than any other.

I could hardly believe my ears as I sat in the prison chapel with the other inmates who worked at MHMR. Mr. Taylor had called us together to notify us of a policy change regarding our jobs, and as I allowed his words to sink in, I wanted to weep and to scream at the same time. He told us that we would soon be required to wear a uniform to work. *A uniform!* I thought. *Then everyone at MHMR will know I'm an inmate!* One of the best things about my job had been the fact that so few people knew. Anonymity had been such a relief.

Upon being informed of the new required dress code, my heart plummeted to my feet and splattered on the floor. My expressionless face betrayed the surge of emotions coursing through me—shock, anger, dread and a fresh wave of the shame I had battled so many times before.

Prison could be so cruel in so many ways, but perhaps none was as painful as being granted some tiny taste of freedom only to have it snatched away. I would have preferred never to enjoy whatever small privilege was given than to savor it for a moment and then lose it. It was like taking one step forward and then three steps backward, and that kind of give-and-take happened all the time.

Although my wardrobe was extremely limited, it was *mine.* Dressed in my civilian clothes, I had begun to feel like a person again and even to sense the first flutters of freedom I had felt since entering prison. My clothes gave me an opportunity to leave behind the stigma that had been forced upon me, and provided a measure of individuality I could never find while dressed in the same colors and styles as every other inmate. But more than that, they effectively hid my legal status and address: federal inmate at the local prison.

At least I did not have to face the challenge alone. For several reasons, I was glad that Charlotte and I were able to work together at MHMR. We enjoyed each other's company for sure, but found that we needed each other's support when it came time to show up at MHMR in our uniforms. Day after day, we encouraged each other by saying, "This too shall pass!"

On the day our new uniforms were issued, I wrote one sentence in my journal.

10/20/95: Got uniforms for MHMR.

I did not have or need any other words. My disappointment over the loss of the small liberty I had known was too deep for description.

The morning finally arrived when I had to wear my new uniform for the first time. It was pink—my least favorite color, which made wearing it doubly difficult. It resembled a medical scrub suit and was to be worn with flimsy white tennis shoes. I did not like anything about it. Dressing for work that day was like robing myself in pink shame. But by the time the workday was over and I had survived my debut as an inmate and finally had a quiet moment in my cell, I pulled out my journal to record what had happened.

> *11/9/95: My Father is so faithful. So hard to explain, but we wore our uniforms for the first time today. My Father had my heart in His hand all day. My attitude has truly and totally changed. It is as if He is showing me His love in a special way. In the prayer closet, He told me how much He loves me. I look so often to the spectacular, but He does speak softly!*

The Holy Spirit spoke softly as He guided my heart through the humiliation of wearing my uniform for the first time. I treasured the intimate relationship He had given me with Himself and knew that only my inner communion with Him had given me the strength to keep from falling apart that day.

As I reflected on my uniform experience and thought about how much I really *had* needed the strength of the Holy Spirit to help me maintain my emotional equilibrium, I remembered another great change that had taken place in me somewhere along the prison path. Before Benton, I had been a slave to my emotions—doing what I felt like doing, going where I felt like going, saying what I felt like saying. Without knowing it, I had given my emotions a frightening amount of control over my actions and influence over my decisions. Emotions kicked me around like a soccer ball and always defeated me.

When I read Hebrews 13:8, which says, "Jesus Christ is the same yesterday, today, and forever," the Holy Spirit gave me a life-changing insight and a key to victory in my everyday existence. He showed me that Jesus' miracle-working power is not only "the same yesterday, today, and forever," but also that Jesus' nature is never-changing. He is stable. He is solid and thoroughly dependable. I realized that Jesus has dominion over His emotions. *If He could live without letting His emotions determine His actions,* I thought, *the Holy Spirit can teach me to live that way too.*

I began a fresh journey through the gospels, looking to see how Jesus conducted Himself in the midst of trying situations, how he handled His anger, how He answered people who needed a compassionate word or touch, how He dealt with fatigue, how He responded to grief and how He held up under pressure and persecution. He was *always* the same, *always* led by the Spirit.

I was so relieved when I realized there was another way to live—being led by the Spirit and not by my emotions! Because I had heard that "we become what we behold," I continued to focus on the stability of Jesus and the more I looked at Him, the more stable I became.

On my first day in pink, the Holy Spirit led me through yet another difficult experience—and He had kept me stable. He had been so near. I had learned by that time that I did not need anything to be easy as long as I knew He was with me, and He certainly was that day. Just before I closed my journal that night, I scribbled a scripture reference: Isaiah 43:2. I did not write the words of the verse, because I knew them in my heart. They had become real to me that day: "When you pass through the waters, I will be with you; and through the rivers, they shall not overflow you. When you walk through the fire, you shall not be burned, nor shall the flame scorch you."

I had made it through the fire of mortal embarrassment in my uniform and, though it wasn't easy, I was not burned. I didn't even smell like smoke.

Chapter 31

Dress Rehearsal

I had thirty-six hours to flirt with freedom. Then again, maybe freedom had thirty-six hours to flirt with me. In late November 1995 (in fact, it was Thanksgiving weekend), I was granted an overnight furlough—an opportunity to leave the prison compound on a Saturday morning and not return until the following evening. Most inmates considered a furlough a privilege, but I found it to be stressful and awkward. I felt like a human boomerang, thrust out into a world I hardly remembered and then suddenly gripped again by the same hands that hurled me out.

My parents made the long drive from Kentucky, eager to visit with me outside of walls and fences and away from the perked-up ears and meddling eyes of guards. Likewise, I looked forward to being with them—and to eating a good, hot meal. When the appointed morning arrived, I did what every inmate does on the day she leaves for furlough—I dressed in the oldest, most worn-out civilian clothes I had. Of course, I only had two choices for everything (pants, shirts, and socks), but I would be able to replace it all while I was out. I knew my parents would take me shopping for new clothes, which I would wear back to Benton and then keep. I had not had new clothes—not a single piece—in almost three years.

When my mother and dad arrived, I was glad to see them, but anxious about my venture into the outside world after being in an institution for so long. I wondered if they knew how nervous I was to be leaving, even if only for thirty-six hours. I realized that they did not, and decided not to tell them.

How could I have truly explained to them what Benton was like? Even though it was a prison, *it was where I lived.* It was its own world, intentionally separated from normal civilian life in more ways than I could ever express. I was accustomed to leaving the compound every weekday for my job at MHMR, but leaving for furlough was different. The same restrictions that made me feel like subhuman government property also formed a strange sort of safety net that ensured a routine that was not always comfortable, but was at least familiar.

Even though I had spent far more of my thirty-five years in the outside world than I had behind bars, the severity of incarceration had changed me. I felt like an awkward misfit, even in my parents' car, as we drove away from a place that should not have felt anything like home, but unexpectedly and uncomfortably, did.

Beyond the boundaries of Benton, all of my five senses shifted into high alert, as the entire outside world seemed to burst into vibrant color and activity when I encountered it— like everything on earth had been in hibernation and erupted with life in one vigorous instant! Of course, nothing in the physical environment had changed at all, but I realized that being in prison had dulled my senses. Being released even briefly allowed me to experience the world as though I had never seen it before.

Benton, Texas was similar to many other small American cities—full of fast-food restaurants, convenience stores, churches, malls, movie theatres, gas stations, hotels, bus stops and anything else a person might need or want. These commonplace shops and services were the fixtures of everyday life for so many people, but to me, each one represented a luxury I had not enjoyed for two years and eleven months.

My parents and I did what countless other families did on Saturdays: we went to the mall. No one—not even I—could have predicted how our afternoon of shopping would impact me. In the mall, I saw a world going very, very fast. I felt as if I had been sitting on a motionless merry-go-round for the past three years and someone had suddenly spun it as fast as it would go. I was astounded by the vast variety and the sheer speed of the activity around me. Shoppers shopped fast; sales clerks sold fast; people with popcorn and soft drinks ate and drank fast; signs blinked on and off fast. To me, mothers even strolled their babies at lightning speed.

In addition to the hustle of the mall, I could hardly believe the dizzying array of items for sale, readily available to anyone willing to pay the price. I was accustomed to a small prison commissary, where choices were a rarity and I had to take whatever they offered.

In the midst of the swirl around me, I realized one of the many silent, debilitating strategies of prison: the removal of a person's power to choose. To me, the worst aspect of not being able to make choices was not that all of the inmates ended up looking alike, but that in many ways, it paralyzed my will. It shut down the function of desire in me because I never had the chance to choose one thing over another or to exercise the simple privilege of saying, "I like that one." Because of that, and because of the frantic pace at which everything and everyone seemed to be moving in the mall, every store and every piece of merchandise presented me with its own fresh, unique intimidation.

To casual observers, my parents and I must have looked like any other family out for an afternoon of shopping. No one could have seen the shame that kept my chin close to my chest or the hidden heartache nestled deep within my mother and dad. No one knew that we had not been in public together for almost three years, and no one knew that I would be locked in prison again by bedtime the next night.

But I knew and my parents knew. In fact, I never really left Benton mentally or emotionally. My body was at the mall, but the rest of me was still in a dorm full of other women who were being punished as criminals. My parents and I were painfully aware that the façade of freedom I had been given would crumble in less than thirty-six hours, and the tension of the ticking clock followed us from store to store, unwanted and unwelcome, but unavoidable.

The highlight of the mall was the squirt of perfume administered by a woman who walked around asking people if they would like to sample a particular fragrance. I did. Nothing ever smelled good in prison—not the food, not the laundry detergent, not the soap or shampoo, not the stale, stagnant air. I especially appreciated pleasant smells and considered the perfume sample an exquisite blessing. While some people seemed to go out of their way to avoid her, I allowed the woman to spray perfume on me, then sniffed my wrists every few minutes as long as the fragrance lingered, basking in the rare treat that other people considered a promotional nuisance. When I could no longer smell it, I went back for another spritz.

Between visits to the woman with the perfume, my mother and I shopped for sunglasses. I found a pair I liked, and noticed a puzzled look on my mother's face as I checked to see how much they cost. When I questioned her expression, she said, "That's the first time I have *ever* seen you look at a price tag."

I never had to look at prices before. For years, I was able to buy whatever I wanted without regard to cost. No more. I made seventeen cents an hour at MHMR; I was still a federal inmate; and I certainly did not have the money for even an inexpensive pair of sunglasses. My mother bought them for me.

My one-day date with liberty was proving more difficult than I ever expected it to be, and I was relieved when my parents and I finally left the mall after purchasing the sunglasses, a new pair of jeans, a new shirt, some new underwear, a new pair of socks, and a new pair of tennis shoes, along with a few personal items I would be allowed to take back into prison.

For dinner that night, my parents and I agreed on a chain restaurant we were all familiar with. To them, it was just another restaurant, but to me it was a battlefield, the scene of another invisible struggle to function in an environment that was so foreign, leftover from another lifetime I remembered but could not re-enter. Once again, the consequences of so many months without being able to choose revealed themselves as I struggled to decide what to order. It had been so long since my plate did not look exactly like every other plate on the table, so long since I had tasted spices and sauces and had food presented attractively and served to me! There was even a sprig of parsley on the edge of my plate, just for the sake of appearance, which looked unusual and seemed frivolous to me now.

The whole day—our trip to the mall, our dinner out—was like a restaurant that only served appetizers. It tantalized my taste for freedom, but offered nothing more than hunger pangs for something I could not have.

That night we stayed in a hotel that could have just as easily been a palace as I reveled in the feel of carpet beneath my feet, the softness of an upholstered chair, the cheerful colors of the bedspreads and curtains. But beyond the visual and tactile benefits of the hotel room was the indefinable opportunity to exercise control: I could lock the door; I could operate the thermostat; and I could even turn the lights off and on when I wanted to. After being subjected for so long to a prison rule or a guard's whim, I turned locks and flicked switches several times *just because I could.*

But nothing felt better to me than the opportunity to bathe in a bathtub, with plenty of hot water, sweet-smelling soap, shampoo and lotion, a heater if I wanted it, and towels that were as soft and fluffy as cotton balls compared to the ones at Benton. On the side of the bathtub, I perched a treat my parents had brought me—a bag of chocolate-covered pretzels, which I treasured in my mouth as though they were edible gold. Above and beyond all that, bath time allowed me to close the bathroom door, which afforded the supreme privilege of all—a moment of true privacy, the height of luxury.

That night, I lay in bed in conflict—grateful for an afternoon with my parents, aware that I was temporarily away from the monotony, other inmates and foul language, thankful for a wonderful bath, glad someone was not tossing and turning in a bed right above me, but acutely aware that it was all fleeting. By the time I awakened the next morning, I would be within several short hours of having to go back to prison for the remainder of my sentence. There would be no more furloughs, no more dress rehearsals. The next time I saw land beyond a prison wall it would be as a free woman, and based on my struggles with things as simple as shopping and eating out, I wondered how freedom would really be once it was a full-time experience.

All three of us, my parents and I, awakened to the tyranny of my necessary return to prison. We checked out of our hotel, attended a local church service and later stopped at a restaurant for dinner, but spent more time watching our watches than we did eating. After all we had been through, I had less than a year left in prison and my parents did not want to break any rules at that point. They were extremely uptight and careful as they monitored the time so they would not be late handing me back to the government.

Back at Benton, when the moment came for the dreaded inevitable, I said goodbye quickly not because I was eager to leave my parents, but to spare all of us a lengthy, more painful farewell. They dropped me off at the R and D building, completely unaware of the check-in procedures I would have to endure in order to be processed back into inmate population. Once inside, I handed my new clothes and other items to a guard so that he could inventory them. And it hit me—as excited as I was to have new things, they really didn't matter. Possessions were still powerless. After another shameful strip search, I walked back to my cell and thought about the thirty-six hours I had been away.

I had courted freedom and freedom had courted me, but it would be months before we would become intimately

acquainted and permanently joined together. If I learned anything from the many experiences and challenges of my furlough, I had learned that I was far more institutionalized than
I thought—and far less prepared to return to civilian life. My
brief venture outside of Benton forced me to declare something I hated to admit: I wasn't ready to be released, and I
probably would not be totally ready when my release day came.
Freedom would be a process, and moving from prison to the
outside world would not be as simple as changing clothes. I
would be trading in an old life for a new one and the adjustment would require more trust, more faith and more preparation than I ever imagined.

Chapter 32

The Basin and the Towel

"Lord, let me serve You fully until the last minute I am here." That was my prayer at the dawn of a new year—1996, the year of my release. Through the winter and early spring, I continued my job at MHMR and did everything I could in order to be prepared for the day I would walk out the doors of the federal prison at Benton as a free woman.

I knew women who had been inmates multiple times in the course of several years because they simply did not know how or were not able to survive in the outside world. Once some of them were released, little time passed before they committed another crime or violated their probation requirements and were sent back to prison. It broke my heart to see these repeat offenders unable to break free of whatever compelled them to constantly choose bondage over freedom. It also told me that life beyond bars could be more difficult than people realized.

I knew that I would not leave prison and intentionally do anything that would send me back—ever. But I was aware, as I had learned on my furlough, that I might find freedom as challenging as some of the repeat offenders had. I was determined to overcome every obstacle and to build a brand-new life on the firm and godly foundation the Holy Spirit was laying in my heart. I focused my energies on being ready to walk in the liberty that would be mine in a matter of months and on serving the Lord in every possible way until the moment I left.

The prison administration demonstrated their intention to release me when they sent me to a pre-release class in April 1996, about nine weeks prior to my scheduled departure date.

> *4/4/96: I had my pre-release class on Wednesday. I remembered the battle I won last month when Veronica went to pre-release. I had to guard my heart from being jealous that her name had appeared on the call-out to go to this class before mine. She was one inmate who certainly wasn't living a "good Christian" example. But that didn't matter. What mattered was the attitude of my heart. I chose to pray and bless Veronica as she announced to everyone that she had made the pre-release list—but it was a battle. Okay. God's timing once again proves perfect!*

The pre-release class was an important step toward helping me really believe I would actually get out of prison someday soon. By that time, I had thought about that day for more than three years, often wondering if it would ever really arrive. I had also been at Benton long enough to know that things changed every day and that many an inmate had completed her pre-release class only to have her hopes dashed days or weeks later by a clerical error, a policy change or a new development in her case. One thing definitely had not changed: things were always changing!

I could hope and pray and believe that nothing would alter my June release, but I still had to capture my thoughts and not let them run ahead of me. Yes, it was all lining up and I was on my way out, but I was not out yet. And I wanted to fully participate in everything that was left for me to do in prison and to learn every last-minute lesson the Holy Spirit wanted to teach me.

Most of all, I wanted to spend time during my few remaining weeks with my friends in the Remnant Group, and the Spirit especially blessed us one night during a meeting:

> *5/4/96: Last night at prayer, God did some great things. This had to be how the early church gathered! We sang and prayed. Laughter, words of healing.*

What a special bunch of inmates we were—the Remnant Group. These were women who had laughed and cried together, worshiped and prayed together, touching far-away nations and unknown people around the world from deep inside a Texas prison camp. We were women who delved into the Word together and encouraged one another in the Lord. We had shared some unique prison joys and fought some unique prison battles together. Yes, I longed for the freedom of being out of prison and not having to return, but I would miss these Remnant Group women—my sisters, my friends.

Friendships are born quickly when people are together in difficulty, and they are forged like iron in the heat of hard places. I could not bear the thought of leaving behind the women in the Remnant Group. Once I stepped off of prison property, I would not be back to visit them; we would not be allowed to talk on the phone; they did not have e-mail access. I would not have the joy of seeing them smile or the comfort of their encouraging words or the simple support of their presence—ever again. Though I knew that the Lord had made us friends forever in Him, the finality of losing the earthly aspects of their friendship was overwhelming.

5/6/96: Last night in my bunk I was hit with emotion. Thinking of Jesus in the garden. Yes, He knew the physical suffering to come, but what about the emotional? He was man. He was leaving people He'd poured His life into, people He'd not really been separated from. Closure was at hand. But Jesus knows and I am not alone.

Once the emotion of leaving hit me, I constantly reminded myself that I was not alone and guarded my mind more diligently against the fear of the future and the fear of being without my friends. I wanted to stay strong for the women around me, but I also knew I had to be honest about the realities within my own heart.

5/28/96: It's coming to a close. It's going to be God's grace that keeps me together to say goodbye to such dear friends. Oh, how I resisted these relationships for so long! How wrong I was. I feel the transition inside. We have an eternity to celebrate the victory, but only a short time to win the battle.

The transition I felt inside was undeniable. Even if I had not had any objective knowledge about my upcoming release, I would have known in my heart that something big was about to happen. Some people would call it "intuition"; others would call it "a sixth sense"; but I knew differently. I knew it was the Lord's hand making my heart ready to leave prison and enter a new season that would take me farther away from government control and closer to ultimate total freedom. And I knew that it was the Lord's voice, speaking to the ears of my heart, whispering the words I would need to cling to through the uncertain days ahead.

5/31/96: So many changes coming . . .

6/7/96: Two weeks and a new season will begin.

As I counted down the last days of my incarceration, I needed the Lord desperately. I needed His encouragement and His strength because, within ten days, I would face enormous change and challenge. He knew, though, and as always, He did not disappoint me.

6/12/96: My heart can only be at such peace because of Jesus. I think about how confident I am leaving—confidence and trust in Him—and there is no pressure or burden on me. Oh, the difference in me since I came to prison!

What a difference indeed. In fact, I would be leaving prison as an entirely different woman than I had been when I arrived, thoroughly changed from the inside out. What wonders I had seen—and what a miracle I was! I had to go to prison to be set free. Imagine that.

With one week left before my release, I completed my job assignment at MHMR and spent my last seven days at Benton anticipating my next phase of freedom.

6/14/96: What a day at work. So emotional saying goodbye. Oh, what a glimpse I have gotten of the power of unconditional love. I saw it break down walls, draw people out of their shells, heal and bind together. Truly, this must be the most excellent way.

As my days at Benton were coming to an end, I heard another piece of news, one that revealed and affirmed again the perfection of God's timing.

6/17/96: This time next week, Dallas. Mr. Gonzalez stopped me today and told me I was lucky. There are not going to be any more work-release programs after mine.

I appreciated Mr. Gonzalez's information, but I certainly did not believe I was "lucky." I didn't believe in luck or fate or chance or the position of the stars or even in coincidence. I believed in the purposes of God and in His perfect timing. If I had just barely made it into the work-release program, it was because the Lord had planned it that way.

Of course, the Lord had planned everything. He was orchestrating my last days as an inmate carefully and allowing me to do just as I had asked, to serve Him and minister to others until I walked out the R and D door.

6/21/96 What a day. I am still praying, "Lord, let me serve You fully until the last minute I am here." As I was packing out, two women came into my cell and started talking. Dedee asked how I had learned to submit to authority. I had only fifteen minutes before I had to report to R and D to turn in my personal belongings so they could be inventoried for my release, but I knew this was a divine opportunity. I had to trust Him to work it out. I felt so vulnerable with all my possessions (not much, but all I had) lying on the floor so exposed. The Spirit strengthened me! I ended up praying with Dedee to receive Jesus into her heart. Glory! I made it to R and D just in time! Later Peggy came to my room. We talked about the Lord, and as she was leaving, I offered to pray for her. Jesus delivered her! She was depressed and confused. She wept as she felt freedom from the Lord fill her.

No question, prison was a difficult environment—lifeless and dreary, even cruel, for most people. It was not a place where joy abounded, but one of the things that truly did bring me joy was watching the Lord touch someone's life. If it was possible to be thrilled in prison, seeing Him heal someone, bless someone or set someone free was what thrilled me. I had only three days before my release and I could not have been given a greater gift than seeing someone receive Jesus and seeing someone delivered from bondage in the midst of my preparations to leave.

The next day was Saturday and the Lord gave me an amazing day of ministry, incredible opportunities to watch Him work in the lives of many inmates. I scheduled appointments with women at the chapel every hour of that day and saw wonder after wonder. At the end of the long day, one more woman asked for prayer.

> *6/22/96: Last night the miracles continued. I met Donna Atkins in the chapel. The Spirit uncovered unforgiveness she held toward her husband since the first week of their marriage (25 years ago!). She prayed, asking for forgiveness and forgiving her husband. Then the Lord blessed us with such a sweet presence.*

Before I left, I wanted to do something special for my friends, something that would let them know how much they meant to me. I prayed, confident that the Holy Spirit would give me an inspired idea. And He did.

I wondered how Jesus must have felt as He prepared to leave His disciples, and I remembered the story in John 13:1-15: ". . . when Jesus knew that His hour had come that He should depart from this world to the Father, having loved His own who were in the world, He loved them to the end . . .

He poured water into a basin and began to wash the disciples' feet and to wipe them with the towel with which He was girded." Then Jesus said, "For I have given you an example, that you should do as I have done to you."

That was what I needed, and wanted, to do. I asked the chaplain if I could use one of the small classrooms off of the chapel on Sunday night. Even though gathering a group of women for an unsupervised meeting was forbidden, she allowed me to use the room. I asked the women of the Remnant Group and several others to meet me there at 7:00 P.M.

I took a small can of orange juice I bought at the commissary and a couple of crackers I borrowed from an inmate. Carrying the silent burden of my impending departure, Liz and I walked to the classroom early. I did not tell her what we were going to do that night, but asked her to be ready to sing when I gave her the cue.

At 7:00 the women arrived, all aware that it was my last night before being released, our final time together. I began by telling them that they had been God's gifts to me while I was in prison, thanked them for their friendship and then shared communion with them. Then, I took a bowl of water and a dingy prison towel, began removing work boots and socks, and washed feet—tired feet, hurting feet, feet that were all walking the uniquely painful path through prison. Praying for each woman as I washed her feet, I asked the Lord to keep revealing His love, to strengthen, to protect and to make known His plans for her life.

Liz sang, and I washed. In my opinion, nobody could sing as sweetly as Liz, especially when she sang about the blood of Jesus; and she sang for more than an hour that night.

By the time it was over, about fifty women had come. With Liz singing, "Oh the blood of Jesus; it washes white as snow," in the background and tears streaming down my face, I asked them to continue doing for others what the Lord had done for them—to comfort those around them who were afraid, to pray for those who needed help and to encourage those who were depressed.

The Lord said, "Yes," to my prayer. He let me serve until the very end. Emotionally and physically exhausted, but profoundly grateful, I took my towel and my bowl and walked toward the dorm with Liz. We walked together to the top of the stairs where I had to turn one way and Liz the other in order to go to our cells. We did not give voice to the gutwrenching goodbyes that lay within our hearts. We hardly said anything at all. It was one of those moments words would have ruined.

Just before the lights went out that night, I crawled into my prison bunk for the last time.

Chapter 33

Half-Way Home

I stood between two lifetimes. Behind me was my life as federal inmate number 22490-077. And before me, well, before me was an unknown existence, an uncharted course, a world from which I had been absent for three-and-a-half years.

It was almost surreal. Even though I had waited for years and known for weeks that today would be the day of my release, still, I could hardly comprehend it. Sometimes there is a fine line between freedom and bondage; but not that day. On that day, the gap was enormous, and I simply did not have the capacity to hold all the thoughts and all the feelings inside of me. *Today I will be a free woman,* I thought. *A free woman.* My journey to freedom had been costly, but it had been worth every heartache and every heartbreak and every hard-fought battle. I wondered what my future would hold, but I could not stand for long at the intersection of uncertainty and ambiguity. I had to get busy preparing to leave prison and to report to a halfway house that afternoon.

Three-and-a-half years previously, I had walked into this prison with a house full of art and furniture and expensive accessories, with a robust stock portfolio and property in Highland Park. I had expected to return to all of that after about a two-week adventure behind bars. Now my house belonged to someone else, the government had liquidated my stock portfolio and the few once-precious possessions I had left were locked in a storage facility somewhere in Texas. I did not even have the money for a bus ticket home. But then again, I did not even know where "home" would be.

On the morning of my release, I had to have my belongings packed and my linens turned in at the laundry room in time to report to the R and D building by 7:30. Everything I had fit into one box—the kind of box that contains paper for copy machines. In the worldly sense, I had truly lost everything. But in another sense, I had gained more than I could have ever asked. I had met the Holy Spirit at Benton. He had guided me in the School of the Spirit and had given some of His choice women to be my classmates and my friends.

As I marveled at the total transformation of my life, my thoughts threatened to de-rail me. I could not let them continue; I had to focus. In spite of the possibility that some last-minute fluke would prevent me from leaving or the fear that I would arrive at R and D only to find out that I could not leave after all, I had to concentrate on going through the motions required for release.

Only a few formalities stood between me and a whole new life, and I had to endure them. I had heard a television preacher say that sometimes we just have "to do things afraid," so I took a deep breath and walked toward R and D. I was not confident and I was not excited; I was terrified.

Inmates transferred in and out of Benton all the time, so the blur of activity surrounding my release was routine, bureaucratic, even mechanical, to the officers there. But as I watched—and participated almost like a robot—I was keenly aware that every bit of the process moved me one step closer to the great and frightening unknown called freedom, aware in the depths of my heart that my life was changing permanently and significantly. I could not think about that, though. I simply had to do what the officials told me to do and lean into the Lord with all of my might. With all the uncertainty ahead of me, I knew there was only one thing I could count on: He would be there.

I filled out forms and signed papers and rubbed my fingers on an inkpad so I could leave behind the necessary set of fingerprints. I stood still for a release photo and answered a series of questions about the personal items I would be taking with me when I left. "Do you have a hairbrush? Do you have a comb? Do you have any toothpaste left?" I was aware enough to know the answers, but stunned enough to only be able to respond with a hollow-sounding "yes" or "no."

Once I completed the necessary paperwork and cooperated with the administrative activities required for my release, an officer informed me, "As soon as your ride comes, you can go." It was that simple. No one really seemed to notice. No fanfare. No tape to run through. No one to hand me a cup of cold water, just an invisible finish line across the end of a grueling, but transforming, journey. With just a few words—a short sentence—I was free to walk out the front doors of R and D and into the world. I lifted my box from the counter and walked slowly, nervously, toward the door, keenly aware that I had no handcuffs chafing my wrists, no shackles weighing down my ankles, no uniform, no I.D. card and no idea what the next phase of my life would hold.

I waited, watching out the R and D window for my sister, who would soon arrive to take me to my next destination—a halfway house in Hudson, Texas, not far from the outskirts of Dallas. I felt like a jittery kindergarten student on her first day of school, filled with many of the same questions and emotions: nervous, awkward, frightened, wondering, "Will I have any friends?" and "What will it be like there?"

When my sister stopped her van in front of the R and D building, I picked up my box, walked out the door and climbed into the front seat. As we drove away from Benton, I was silent, overwhelmed. I did not want to talk. I did not know what to say.

I had to report to the halfway house four hours after we left Benton, and the drive would take about three-and-a-half hours. I wondered if we would stop to eat. We did stop at a fast-food restaurant and, just as I had been during my furlough, I was totally unprepared for everything I encountered there. The menu boards were bright and colorful and the restaurant was full of windows and light. The sizzle and smell of frying hamburgers filled the air, and everywhere I looked, people were moving about freely, happily, seemingly without a care in the world. In contrast to the slow, heavy pace of prison, everything in the restaurant seemed to move at the speed of sound and I was completely taken aback by the whole experience.

My eyes were not accustomed to the pictures and the colors I saw as I read the menu. But more than that, except on my furlough, I had not been able to choose my own food for more than three years. I was mentally paralyzed as I tried to decide whether to order a hamburger or a chicken sandwich.

Finally, confused and unable to process any more stimuli, I managed to place an order for something I was not even sure I wanted.

I had done my best to prepare to leave Benton, knowing that moving back into the free world would be challenging. But I had not known my struggles would begin at a hamburger restaurant! After having been gone from prison less than four hours, I could tell that the path ahead of me would be more difficult than I ever imagined.

Right on time, we pulled into the driveway of the halfway house, which was located in the middle of a cornfield, behind a chain-link fence. I would spend the next year of my life there while I satisfied the work-release requirement that was part of my prison sentence. Filled with uncertainty, I had already experienced more than enough sensory and emotional overload for one day, and did not look forward to having to meet new people and adjust to new living conditions. I just wanted nighttime to come so I could go to bed.

I had never heard a good report about a halfway house, and as I walked into the one I would be living in, I could see why! Immediately, a woman inventoried my belongings and requested a urine sample. She then led me to a room that housed about sixteen women, where she showed me my bunk, my locker and the two restrooms shared by everyone in the room.

But one of the first things I noticed was that the halfway house was not only for women. Men lived there too. I had not lived around men for three-and-a-half years, and assumed the men had not lived around women either. Of course, Benton had employed a number of male guards and prison officials, so I had interacted with men. But I had not lived in the same house with them, and I found the arrangement unsettling. I had not completed my first day at the halfway house before I decided that my living conditions had not improved as much as I thought they would.

I thought about Ashfield and observed, *At least it's better than that.* I remembered thinking while I was there that, if I could find God there, I could find Him anywhere. I knew that He had not left me alone, that He was as near to me at the halfway house as He had ever been. I simply needed to hear His voice and allow Him to give me a strategy for living in this unnerving new situation.

For the next few days, I was not allowed to leave the facility, even to go to work, so I stayed fairly quiet and planted my feet firmly on the path I knew would lead to victory—much prayer, much time in the Word, much diligence to guard my thoughts, obeying the house rules, constantly leaning on the Holy Spirit.

I never felt at ease in the halfway house. I knew other women who had been sent back to prison from this facility for breaking the rules, so I lived with a continual undercurrent of anxiety as I wondered if I might be sent back too. One day, a Marshal's car pulled into the driveway and terror gripped my heart as I wondered, *Are they here for me? Did I do something wrong? Are they taking me back to prison?* Thank goodness! They were there for someone else, someone whose urinalysis had tested positive for drug use. I began to breathe again as I realized they were not going to take me anywhere. They were not there for me at all.

As difficult as the halfway house was, I had to keep reminding myself that it was only a temporary stopping place on the road to eventual freedom. I *had* to do time in a halfway house, and I just wanted to get it over with.

The Holy Spirit revealed strategies to help me live there and established a rhythm of grace for that new season. One of the biggest adjustments was having to live apart from my Christian friends. I missed them terribly and loneliness threatened to engulf me. We had shared so much. They didn't even know where I was, but I knew they missed me (I had lost friends to freedom before too), and I knew they were praying. I desperately wanted to see my friends but I had to keep reminding myself that I was not really alone, and I retreated over and over again to the everlasting arms of the Lord—the only one who could reach me in that halfway house in Hudson, Texas.

I was soon more settled, but no more comfortable in my circumstances. Once again, the Lord had not removed me from difficulty, but once again, He was giving me victory in the midst of a battle.

6/96: Here I sit at the halfway house in a quiet room designated as the chapel. Already it seems so long ago—Benton/ prison only a few hours' drive away, yet a totally different world now.

The halfway house was indeed a different environment than Benton but was more closely related to prison than it was to the free world. This reality struck me in a powerful way after I had been there several weeks, when I was eligible for an eight-hour furlough one Saturday, for which my sister took me to her house.

When I walked through the door, the sights and smells and comforts of a home overwhelmed me. The warm colors and cozy furnishings of her house surprised my eyes, which were still unaccustomed to beauty. But what startled me most was the moment I took a seat on her sofa. As I sank into the cushions, I realized that I had not sat on anything so soft in a long, long time.

After a good day together, we headed back to the halfway house and during the forty-five minute drive, stopped at a convenience store for a soft drink. Little did I know, this seemingly routine activity became a venue in which the Holy Spirit revealed another one of the astounding works He had done while I was in prison. Inside the store, I bumped head-on into an old foe—all sorts of alcoholic beverages and attractive displays of wine bottles. It had been a long while since I had seen alcohol, and this was the first time it had been within arm's reach since before I went to prison.

The displays, of course, were designed to entice people to purchase, but for the first time in my life, I was not enticed at all. Alcohol had lost its grip on me! God's power had freed me from that formerly inescapable temptation. Alcohol once had power over me, but now I had power over it. With a huge grin on my face and a bottle of water in my hand, I left the convenience store with my heart rejoicing in this most recent victory.

Chapter 34

Every Path Leads to Life

My time at the halfway house was not easy but did provide an opportunity for me to re-awaken to the outside world from which I had been severed for so long. Prison was not the most progressive place on earth, and after my release I truly found myself living in a whole new world.

Countries and governments that existed when I went into prison had vanished, and new nations with new names had taken their place. Arts and entertainment and the media were different. But above all, technology had exploded, and that affected my next step into freedom more than anything else.

The work-release program was a three-way arrangement between Benton, the halfway house and the Veteran's Administration Hospital in Dallas, which became my first place of "employment." Just when it was time for me to begin working, the hospital created a new position: receptionist in the chapel. I got the job and received a substantial raise—from seventeen cents per hour at Benton to fifty cents per hour as the chapel receptionist! But before starting those duties, I was required to complete a two-week training program designed to help inmates acclimate to the hospital and either learn or refresh the skills necessary for their jobs.

The software programs my supervisor wanted me to learn were like foreign languages to me. I felt as though I were standing in the middle of a technological tower of Babel—unable to understand anything that computer was trying to say. But technology was only one area in which I was totally overwhelmed by the life activities that were common, everyday functions to most other people around me.

Then again, activities that were common, everyday functions to most other people were, for me, new levels of freedom and testing. I could not describe how totally free I felt when I was able to go to the hospital cafeteria for lunch or to the gift shop during my break time. Visits to the gift shop quickly became one of my favorite activities, as I browsed around the little store that not only carried small gifts, but a limited selection of clothing as well. Bright colors were still a delight to my eyes, but more than that, I loved the fabrics. As if I were touching priceless treasures, I ran my hands over the various textures of material—the tiny bumps on a golf shirt, the cool softness of a silky scarf, the smooth, polished metal of a belt buckle.

The "sameness" of prison had woven itself into my life over the years, and could only be unraveled one stitch at a time. The variety in the gift shop, the choice of foods on the cafeteria's vast smorgasbord, being able to decide what to wear to work each day—all the little options gradually became more comfortable, but I did not take them for granted.

With freedom came testing, and they came in the same package—the V.A. Hospital. Because the hospital was large enough for some of the inmates in the work-release program to easily find a location where they would not be seen, they often met friends or family members during their lunch breaks—in blatant violation of the halfway house rules. Many times, I was pressured to join in these activities and encouraged to get a cellular telephone and hide it at work. That way, they said, I could make unmonitored phone calls, which the rules of the program strictly prohibited.

In the face of those temptations, I remembered that having an excellent spirit means doing the right thing when nobody is looking—but my increased liberties intensified the pressure to cut corners and break rules. The Bible was always an effective weapon, but I could not look up a verse to counteract each temptation as it arose. Instead, I depended on the Word that had been deposited in my heart while in prison and I depended on the Spirit to walk me through every trying situation.

After twelve months at the hospital and gaining proficiency on the computer, I had completed the work-release requirements, and it was time to find a job of my own. I was also eligible to leave the halfway house and transition to house arrest, if I could provide proof of a place to live. My first priority was to find another job because, before I could pay rent, I had to make some money—and it had to be more than fifty cents per hour.

As part of my job search, the first person I contacted was my friend Dr. Gee, the OB/GYN who had treated me for years and cared for me throughout my bizarre experience with the blighted ovum. She knew my story well—the pharmacy days, the trial, the conviction and the prison term. At that time, I believed I would be able to return to practicing pharmacy, and Dr. Gee provided some helpful leads that seemed certain to materialize.

In the midst of want ads and resumes and interviews, I received a phone call from Gary, the same Gary whom the Lord had sent to Benton when He wanted to drastically change my life. Once again, the Lord had a message for me through Gary. He called to tell me that he had been praying for me and encouraged me to seek employment at Bill Glass Ministries. *Bill Glass Ministries*, I thought, *what is that?* I was still not sure what the Lord wanted me to do for employment, but I respected Gary enough to at least explore this unexpected option. After praying, I decided to put my pharmaceutical pursuits on hold and contacted that ministry.

They asked me to come for an interview, which was easier said than done because I did not have a car; I did not have much money; and their office was about a thirty-minute drive from the halfway house. I spent all but a dollar on cab fare getting to the interview and had no idea how I would get back to the halfway house when it was over.

I interviewed with the chief financial officer, a kind, easy-going man named John Worley. To my surprise, he never asked about my typing skills, my computer abilities or my work experience. He simply wanted to know my story. So I shared with him my journey prior to and during my prison term. He listened and asked me to return soon for a second interview with two other executives.

I thanked John for his time and prepared to leave, knowing I had no way to get back to the halfway house. It was going to be a long walk! As I turned and moved toward the door, John stopped me by saying, "Do you need a ride back to the halfway house?" What a relief! He could not have possibly known I was almost broke.

During the ride, John asked me where I planned to go to

church when I was free to do so. I had not been allowed to leave the halfway house to even attend a church service by that time, so I said, "I have no idea." Then he began to tell me about the church he attended, Sojourn Church, in the north Dallas area—and something about it sounded strangely familiar.

Suddenly, I remembered a letter I received before I left Benton, a letter from Gary's friend Mark, the same friend who had prayed for us during that life-changing visit. I had written Mark earlier and asked him to recommend a church in Dallas. He had responded in a letter that read, "I don't recommend churches; I recommend people. And I highly recommend Terry and Susan Moore at Sojourn Church." I had that letter in my purse, which was most unusual because I rarely kept anything, certainly not a letter for six months! *This is no coincidence!* I thought.

Within two weeks, I interviewed with Bill Glass Ministries a second time and they offered me a job. *This is great*, I thought, *only one more obstacle before I can get out of this halfway house*. Next on my list—find a place to live. Taking the job at the ministry would mean that I could not pursue any of the employment options I had discussed with Dr. Gee. *Maybe the timing isn't right yet for me to return to the medical field*, I thought. The ministry job seemed to be the Lord's next step for me, so I decided to work there while pursuing the reinstatement of my pharmacist's license.

When I called Dr. Gee to tell her what I had decided, the Lord put into place the last piece I needed in order to move forward. In the course of our phone conversation, I told her that I would be able to leave the halfway house within several weeks if I could find another place to live. Dr. Gee had an idea and, before too long, arrangements were made for me to live in an apartment with her friend, Mrs. Jefferson, an elderly, bedridden woman who needed someone nearby at night.

I moved out of the halfway house and entered a six-month period of house arrest. During that time, I was forbidden to leave Dallas County and required to keep the authorities at the halfway house informed of my whereabouts because, technically, I was still under their jurisdiction. I had to give them a percentage of my wages, and observe a 9:00 P.M. curfew every night. I even had to call the halfway house and report when I left my job for lunch, call when I returned from lunch, call when I left to go home for the day, and call again when I arrived at Mrs. Jefferson's apartment.

On the weekends, during my time of house arrest, I performed the difficult but necessary task of cleaning out the two storage units where all of my possessions had been stashed when the presidential pardon was not granted. At that time, my accountant oversaw the sale of my house and the moving of everything in it to those storage units.

I needed to empty them as quickly as possible because the lease would soon expire, and I approached the task as something that just had to be done. I spent hours sifting through my relics alone, but one weekend John Worley volunteered himself and his family to help. John, his wife, Nancy, and their two children met me on a Saturday morning and spent the better part of the day assisting me. I was glad to have the extra arms and legs and thankful for the opportunity to get to know the Worleys.

Over the following weekends, I realized that emptying the storage units was a larger job than I ever imagined. I had known it would be time-consuming, but I did not realize that, in the cleaning out, I would find myself spending hours and hours re-living my life. Weekend after weekend, I sorted through two storage units full of old memories, each one tugging on the strings of my heart and demanding a decision: hold on or let go.

Because many of my belongings were ruined after four-and-a-half years in storage, I had a large pile of things fit only for the trashcan. I donated what could be salvaged to a group of refugees—tables, chairs, mattresses, sofas, appliances.

I did not expect to have the money to buy another house any time soon, but that was not the only reason I donated so much. Everything I had felt like props left over from a bad movie. Most of it brought back negative and painful memories and did not reflect my new life. I had bought these things while I was still living in darkness and bondage, and I did not want to be surrounded by souvenirs of a past I was determined to leave behind. Post-prison, I wanted a fresh start in every way, even if it meant not having anything for a while. I could certainly trust and believe the Lord to furnish a small apartment when it was time for me to move out on my own.

That would not take too long, I concluded, after my license was reinstated and I could go back to work as a pharmacist, with a substantial salary increase. For that reason, I contacted the State Board of Pharmacy in Austin and they scheduled a hearing for me. *This is encouraging,* I thought. *The minute they hand my license back, I am on my way.*

After obtaining permission from the authorities at the halfway house, I drove to Austin and arrived early for my scheduled appointment. For three hours, I sat on a bench outside the room where the board was hearing cases. I watched pharmacist after pharmacist enter the room for their hearings, and as they did, I silently prayed for them. I saw each one exit with smiles on their faces, obviously pleased by the board's positive action.

The committee finally admitted me as their last appointment before the lunch break. I appeared before them full of confidence, believing that my license would be restored, and that this hearing was only a formality on my way back behind the counter. The instant I took my seat, my confidence was shattered. It was like reliving my criminal trial. Some of the same people who had testified against me then were in the room that day, launching a fresh onslaught of brutal accusations. I felt as though I were being prosecuted all over again. They made their decision quickly. They refused to reissue my license and announced that it was time to eat.

Shocked by the board's action and surprised by their decision, I caught the first available elevator to the ground floor so that I could get out of the building as fast as possible. Stepping onto it, I instantly found myself in the company of the entire pharmacy board.

The Holy Spirit spoke to me and said, "Turn around and thank them for their time today." I could not imagine anything more difficult—or more awkward. But I knew He had spoken. So I turned around, faced the board, and said, "Thank you all for your time today."

No one said a word.

After a few moments that seemed like years, the elevator doors opened and we went our separate ways—forever. My pharmacy career was decisively finished.

I sat in the car, stunned and terribly confused. Remembering a moment in prison when I believed the Holy Spirit had spoken to me and promised to restore everything, I said to Him, "But why? You promised to restore all!" I did not understand and I did not want to talk about it any more. I had made plans to meet some friends for lunch, so I pulled out of the parking garage and headed for the restaurant.

When I arrived, two friends, Donna and David were waiting for me. With them was a young man named George, whom I had never met. They knew I had been in an important meeting, and I found it odd that they did not even inquire about its outcome. I wanted them to ask so that I could pour out my frustrations and express my pitiful selfish attitude. But the Holy Spirit had other things on His heart.

The minute I looked at George, the Holy Spirit gave me revelation into his life. He showed me specific things that had happened to him as a child, and told me what to say to him. The Holy Spirit had a specific message for him that day, a message to help heal the pain of his past—and He wanted me to speak it.

The Holy Spirit and I had a silent conversation about His request.

No. I don't want to tell him anything. I want to talk about my meeting, I said.

Tell him, the Holy Spirit said.

But I want to talk about what happened to me this morning.

Tell him, the Holy Spirit repeated for the third time.

Reluctantly, I took my focus off of myself and began to encourage George by sharing what the Holy Spirit had spoken to me about his life. He was moved to tears, and those words seemed to bring healing to some old wounds—deep places that had festered inside of him for a long time. I might have lost my right to dispense medicine, but the Holy Spirit still had plans to use me to bring healing to others.

By the time lunch ended, not a single word had been spoken about *my* future. As we were leaving the restaurant, David pulled me aside and said that he and his wife had been praying, and that the Holy Spirit had told them to give me something. He handed me an envelope. I thanked him, slipped the envelope into my purse, said good-bye and headed back to Dallas. Just as I was leaving the city of Austin, I opened the envelope from David and pulled out a check, made out to me. Provision from an unexpected source.

Suddenly, I was overwhelmed with the presence of the Holy Spirit. It was as if He totally flooded my car and said, "Your family and friends will view the failure to get your pharmacist's license back as a major defeat, just as the world viewed Jesus on the cross as a major defeat. But," He said, "I'm telling you that today is a great victory. I will provide for you." David's check was proof positive of the Lord's promise to provide at a moment when I desperately needed it. I did not know what the next step on my journey would be, but I did know that, with the Lord charting my course, every path would lead to life.

Chapter 35

Beginning Again

That Sunday morning, for most people, was probably just like any other. But not for me. I was going to church. After all I had heard about it, I was eager to visit Sojourn Church and that was exactly where I was headed.

Dressed in my very best outfit, I made my way through the check-out process at the halfway house—signing out, writing down where I was going and promising to return four hours later. *A church bulletin*, I said to myself, *I've got to remember to bring back a church bulletin.* One of the rules at the halfway house was that whenever anyone was granted a pass on Sunday morning, that person was required to show a church bulletin to the authorities as proof of church attendance. Some people spent their four hours doing anything but going to church and simply stopped by a convenient house of worship just long enough to run in and grab the necessary evidence!

Not me. I really wanted to go to church that morning and had made arrangements with Laurel, a friend from Dallas, to pick me up at the halfway house and drive me to Sojourn. Waiting and watching for her to arrive, I was excited, even thrilled, but also extremely nervous.

Laurel and I pulled into the parking lot just as the service began. Two questions battled for first place in my mind. A nagging wonder: "Can people tell that I just got out of prison?" And, the most important issue—a question in the form of a prayer: "Lord, is this really the church where you want me to be?"

As soon as I walked in the front door, the Holy Spirit spoke to me and said, "The love of the Father is here to heal you." I realized that He had gone before me, and I found great comfort in walking into a place I had never been before and feeling that I had been there all of my life.

The music had already started by the time Laurel and I entered the sanctuary, and as we did, I was shocked by what I saw and heard. I saw happy people, praising the Lord unashamedly, with smiling faces and upraised hands. And I heard upbeat, contemporary music that reminded me of the music at the revival service in my hometown more than twenty years earlier. At Benton, the only instruments that accompanied our songs of worship were Ben's guitar and an occasional out-of-tune piano. The music had been sweet and pure, with its own unique loveliness, but this was different. My ears snapped to full attention, surprised by the volume and energy of the keyboards and drums and basses and guitars all flowing through an excellent sound system in joyful, vibrant rhythm and harmony.

Besides that, the church did not have any pews. I had never seen comfortable, padded chairs in a church before. I had to adjust to the unexpected furnishings, and decided instantly that I liked them. When the music was over and we settled into our seats, a pastor stepped to the microphone and welcomed visitors, asking first-time guests to raise their hands. When the woman next to me realized I had never been there before, she leaned over and said with a gentle smile, "Oh honey, I'm sorry, this is Missions Sunday. I do hope you'll give us another try sometime!"

Missions Sunday or not, I knew that I would not need to give Sojourn Church another try. The Holy Spirit had obviously led me there and spoken so clearly the instant I stepped into the building. I did not have to make a decision; I simply had to follow His leading. I knew I was home and the next step would be to get to know my family.

That first Sunday, Laurel and I had to leave early so that I would not be late for the halfway house curfew, and we did not have time to meet anyone. I did see the pastor, Terry Moore, even though he did not preach that morning. I also noticed a family among the crowd—a husband and wife and two daughters—who caught my eye for some reason I did not understand.

I continued going to Sojourn and, before too long, the Lord began to give me friends there just as He had done with Liz and others at Benton. One Sunday, Terry Moore introduced himself because he recognized me as someone new. He did not know how "new" I was! Certainly my life had been made new in prison because of my experiences with the Holy Spirit, but I was also brand new to even the most routine aspects of church life—like being spoken to by the pastor. I was so conscious of my recent past, as I tried to walk in new "shoes" of shame I had never worn before—the humiliation and awkward feelings of rejection that came with being an ex-con in the free world.

I struggled socially perhaps more than anything else, which reminded me again that I was more institutionalized than I realized. It took months for me to gain any measure of comfort in meeting new people because I did not know how to relate to people outside of prison and felt that they had no frame of reference for relating to me. The chasm between prison life and freedom was too wide for me to reach across.

Hopefully, none of my new acquaintances would be going to prison, so I knew I would be the one who needed to make the adjustments in order to develop relationships. I saw again how critical it was for the Lord to choose my friendships, to connect me with the right people and to allow Him to develop those relationships at His pace and to whatever depth He had designed. As unsteady as I was wading into the whole area of relationships, I knew I could trust the Holy Spirit to lead and teach me.

He did indeed lead me into relationships with two families at Sojourn. I ended up meeting the family who caught my eye the first time I visited the church: Steve and Melody Dulin and their two daughters, Kristin and Kassie. Their hearts were wide open to me and, though they knew I had been in prison, they never treated me that way. Without my knowledge, the Lord had assigned me to them and to Melody's parents, who had been in prison ministry for many years, as a prayer project before we ever met each other. They took their assignment seriously, never prying into my life, but genuinely wanting to know and understand my challenges so that they could pray specifically for me as I walked through my struggles and faced my fears.

I also became acquainted with Terry and Susan Moore and immediately saw in Terry a deep gift of godly humility and in Susan an abiding gift of gentle grace. I found them to be lovers of God's Word, with hearts that beat to help other people. They befriended me and began to mentor me every way they could, helping to ease my transition into church life and social settings.

One of the qualities about them that meant so much to me was that they could see quickly beyond everything—my past, my time in prison, the shame I still carried—straight to God's call on my life. They could perceive His larger purposes for me and did everything within their power to encourage and assist me to discover and pursue God's destiny for my life. I heard so much of what the Holy Spirit had taught me in the words they spoke and realized that the truth He had deposited in me resonated with the truth that was rooted in their hearts. What a confirmation that I was indeed in the right place, at the right time, with the right people.

Months later, the Holy Spirit showed me a scripture to help me understand that He had done more for me than just provide helpful friends. He had performed the promise of Psalm 68:6: "God sets the solitary in families." Where my time in prison had focused on just "God and me," once I got out, He began to teach me more and more how much He uses other people. He showed me again that I needed them, they needed me and that He could and would use all of us in each other's lives.

But going to church was only one of my weekend activities, because I was still in the process of cleaning out the storage units. One weekend, I had almost finished emptying out the last one when I noticed a box in the far right corner. I thought I had gone through all of my boxes by that time, and I did not remember seeing this one before. But the moment I opened it, a tidal wave of emotions swept over me. Inside, carefully packed, was everything I had purchased for

my wedding—gifts for the flower girls, gifts for my brides-
maids, the ring bearer's pillow. It was all still there, in good
condition—the remains of a wedding that never happened.

I began to weep. Every tear was packed with pent-up
emotion and came from a deep place that had been closed
and locked for years. With my box in tow, I managed to drive
to John and Nancy Worley's house and collapse. For forty-
five minutes I lay on their living room floor, curled in a fetal
position crying hysterically. The process of releasing the pain
seemed un-survivable. John and Nancy prayed, and at last, I
regained my composure long enough to explain my mysterious box I had carried into their home.

Perhaps my grieving was the last release I needed before I could take the next step on the journey of my life.
Within several weeks, my period of house arrest would be
completed, and I would be able to rent an apartment of
my very own. I was overcome as I thought of what a mile-
stone having an apartment would be. Having my own place
would mark the end of a long and difficult season, but a
season I would not have missed for anything in the world.
It was time to start all over, to start "from scratch." It was
like standing on the edge of the bird's nest again at the
opening of a whole new life, and I could not find words
to express the bubbling anticipation and the deep-flow-
ing gratitude in my heart.

Excited and a bit nervous, I looked all over north Dallas,
knowing by then that I wanted to live fairly close to my church
and close to the people who were becoming my friends. Leas-
ing an apartment is not easy when a person is a convicted
felon, but after weeks of searching, I finally found a small
one-bedroom, third-floor unit in the only complex that would
rent to me.

I could hardly believe it when the day arrived for me to move into my first place of real privacy in more than five years. It was a far cry from my house in Highland Park, but it was an even further cry from a prison cell.

My sister and a friend helped me move in, which did not take long because I did not have very much. They left quickly, perhaps sensing how excited I was to have my own place again, but probably not able to comprehend how profoundly grateful I was.

I thanked them for their help and closed the door behind them, keenly aware of the weight of that moment and the long journey that had brought me to it. I turned to my left, where most of the wall was a window and a sliding glass door. A view. I had a view. I had glass, see-through glass, glass I could look out of and see trees. For three-and-a-half years at Benton I had peered through a tiny window and looked at the same red institutional roof. How I had longed to look out and see green—and now I could!

I was exhausted from moving and I hardly had any furniture, so I sat down on the floor with tears of gratitude streaming down my face, looking out at my new view when the Holy Spirit said, "Mary, thanks for waiting."

Only He knew how long I had waited and how painful the waiting process had been at times. Only He knew the seeds of prayer I had sown into other people's lives as I had often prayed for other inmates to be moved to better cells or to prisons where they would be closer to family or where the labor would be less strenuous. So many times, I had wanted Him to move me, but He required me to stay right where I was. Until now.

I had similar thoughts to ones I had recorded years earlier, after I had been in prison almost one year.

1/7/94: Dear Lord, I have no idea what You have in my tomorrow. But through this, I know I can trust You. Thank You for choosing me to walk this path. Your grace will not be in vain.

Love,
Mary

Epilogue

The bus bounced along a dusty road somewhere outside of Buenos Aires, Argentina. Excitement was buzzing behind me as people all around anticipated the next stop on our mission trip. But I paid no attention to anything other than my own thoughts.

"You're awfully quiet," observed the man sitting next to me. "What's the matter? Never been in a prison before?"

"Oh, I've been in a prison before. I lived in one for several years."

Silence in the seat beside me.

Not wanting to talk, but trying to relieve the awkwardness of the moment, I continued, "I'm the speaker today."

The fact that I was on my way to speak to a group of inmates at a women's prison was no small wonder. As a condition of my probationary period, Judge Faulk had ordered me not to leave Dallas County. I was not even allowed to visit my parents in Kentucky, but my request to go to Argentina was approved without the slightest hassle. I wondered why the judge had granted me special permission to travel an entire continent away from home, but knew, of course, that there was only one reason. The Lord was sending me to the prison that day with a message of hope for the women incarcerated there.

My mind wandered from memory to memory as the bus rolled slowly through the prison gates. I remembered the first time I rode into Benton—arrogant, defiant and feeling infinitely superior to everyone there. I remembered the devastation I felt when my promised pardon was denied. And I remembered many of the incredible lessons I had learned in my School of the Spirit. I had thought, from time to time, about how to summarize my behind-bars experiences with the Holy Spirit and everything He had taught me. I could do it in six words: Jesus loves me, *this I know.*

It was His love that gave me the strength to walk back into a prison that day. My heart nearly burst with compassion for the inmates and I was deeply aware of the God-given privilege that was mine—to share hope, to speak encouragement, and with the help of the Holy Spirit, to even utter words of truth and grace that could change an inmate's life.

A guard's voice pulled me back to the present moment as he instructed me to walk through the security screening device and motioned me into the prison. I gulped. "It's all right, Mary," the Holy Spirit whispered. "You can do this." Recalling the miraculous leniency of Judge Faulk in allowing me to be there and believing that the Lord had sent me, I agreed. "Yes, Holy Spirit. I can do this. No; *we* can do this."

Even though I knew I was thousands of miles away, I might as well have been back at Benton as I realized that a prison is a prison and captivity is captivity, no matter what its location. I also knew that people are people and pain is pain. But the truth that supercedes those realities is that freedom is freedom and that the Holy Spirit longs to minister liberty to everyone.

I knew He wanted to set captives free in that Argentine prison that day and He was allowing me to be His mouthpiece. After all, I had a great deal of credibility with my audience as soon as I told them that I too had once worn a prison uniform and answered to a number. Even though we did not speak the same language, we had so much in common. Through a translator, I spoke the words the Lord had given me that day. But I knew that the real translator in our midst was the Holy Spirit and that only He could take the little sparks of my message and build a bonfire in a human heart.

Since that day, other opportunities have arisen for me to share the story the Lord has written on the tablet of my life. Whether I look into the lens of a television camera or into the eyes of a church congregation or into the hearts of prisoners, the message is the same: Jesus loves *you*, this I know.

NOTES

1. Corrie ten Boom with Jamie Buckingham, *Tramp for the Lord* (Fort Washington, PA: Christian Literature Crusade and Old Tappan, NJ: Fleming H. Revell Company, 1974), 80-81.

2. Corrie ten Boom with John and Elizabeth Sherrill, *The Hiding Place* (Washington Depot, CT: Chosen Books, 1971), 183.

3. Ibid, 202.

4. Ibid, 197.

5. Ibid, 203.

6. Ibid, 193-194.

7. Jamie Buckingham, *Daughter of Destiny* (South Plainfield, NJ: Bride Publishing, 1976), 89, 91.